A Practical Guide to Working with Reluctant Clients in Health and Social Care

of related interest

Being White in the Helping Professions
Developing Effective Intercultural Awareness
Judy Ryde
Foreword by Colin Lago
ISBN 978 1 84310 936 5

Effective Communication
A Workbook for Social Care Workers
Suzan Collins
ISBN 978 1 84310 927 3
Knowledge and Skills for Social Care Workers

Recording Skills in Safeguarding Adults
Best Practice and Evidential Requirements
Jacki Pritchard with Simon Leslie
ISBN 978 1 84905 112 5

Relationship-Based Social Work
Getting to the Heart of Practice
Edited by Gillian Ruch, Danielle Turney and Adrian Ward
ISBN 978 1 84905 003 6

The Survival Guide for Newly Qualified Child and Family Social Workers
Hitting the Ground Running
Helen Donnellan and Gordon Jack
ISBN 978 1 84310 989 1

The Art of Helping Others
Being Around, Being There, Being Wise
Heather Smith and Mark Smith
ISBN 978 1 84310 638 8

A Practical Guide to Working with Reluctant Clients in Health and Social Care

Maggie Kindred

Illustrated by Cath Kindred

Jessica Kingsley *Publishers*
London and Philadelphia

Epigraph on p.27 reprinted with permission from the C.S. Lewis Company.
List on pp.81–82 adapted with permission from Gloucestershire Hospitals NHS Trust 2003.
'Mr and Mrs Sunderland' exercise adapted with permission from Doel and Shardlow 2005.
'Other people's records!' exercise adapted with permission from Doel and Shardlow 1993.

First published in 2011
by Jessica Kingsley Publishers
116 Pentonville Road
London N1 9JB, UK
and
400 Market Street, Suite 400
Philadelphia, PA 19106, USA

www.jkp.com

Library of Congress Cataloging in Publication Data
Kindred, Maggie, 1940-
A practical guide to working with reluctant clients in health and
social care / Maggie Kindred ; illustrated by Cath Kindred.
p. cm.
Includes bibliographical references and index.
ISBN 978-1-84905-102-6 (alk. paper)
1. Involuntary treatment. 2. Social service. 3. Medical care. I. Title.
R727.35.K56 2010
362.1--dc22
2010016276

British Library Cataloguing in Publication Data
A CIP catalogue record for this book is available from the British Library

ISBN 978 1 84905 102 6

Printed and bound in Great Britain by
MPG Books Group

Acknowledgements

To all my clients and colleagues with great affection and respect. This book only exists because of them.

To my partner Michael, for laughing at the humorous bits, and all his wonderful 'behind the page' support.

To my daughter Cath for her creativity and scientific outlook, which have been so valuable.

To social workers Jennifer Fox and Janet Scott for their honest feedback.

To Nigel Horner for his gifted teaching, which has enhanced my own practice.

Thank you Steve Jones and Caroline Walton at Jessica Kingsley Publishers for your wonderful encouragement and patient feedback – I have learned so much.

Contents

1. Starting Points

We all start somewhere different…

…so how do we find our way?

INTRODUCTION – HELPING EACH OTHER

Perhaps we find our way best by working with those who challenge us the most. I have personally found that clients who have not chosen to be service users are the most challenging, and therefore the most rewarding to work with. I feel sorry that such people are often disliked and sometimes feared, and hope that my positive experiences may be worth sharing with others who are also finding their way as workers.

So who are the involuntary clients? They are usually people who are defined by *others* to be in some sort of need. There is a spectrum of reluctance, from the ambivalence which most of us have about receiving treatment, whilst freely acknowledging the need for it, through to the groups of people who really are there by force, namely prisoners, adults who have harmed children, people with mental illness whose reality sense is impaired, and older clients who need help with everyday living for the first time in their lives. I would also include people with a whole range of disabilities which place them on the books of professionals for their entire lives.

The book is primarily for practitioners in health and social care in the broadest sense: all workers who try to make relationships with people who do not want help. It is therefore also a relevant title for informal carers and volunteers, who often provide 'hands on' services to the above groups with very little support or recognition.

I have chosen to call the service users 'clients' even though it is a rather formal term; in my opinion it is the most respectful way to describe receivers of services. About clients: I believe that we are not 'friends' to anyone whom we are helping in a professional context, or in a situation which has similar characteristics, for example being a carer to someone who is not a member of your family, and whom you have met through an organisation which exists to respond to needs such as theirs.

Blurring the distinction between friendship and this other kind of help usually leads to misunderstanding, and can do actual harm. However, a whole range of new possibilities and challenges emerges when you undertake such special work, because it is not 'loaded' with the highly charged emotions which develop in your personal or family relationships. This has been called 'skilled helping' (Egan 1994), because most of us find that training is useful in dealing with the challenges and possibilities – hence books like this!

USING THE BOOK

There are many books about the helping process, but few which promote a light-hearted and easily digested approach to the subject matter. The issues faced by clients and workers are far from 'light';

they are sad, painful, dangerous and taxing. However, I have found that letting fun and learning go hand in hand succeeds better than the formality of textbooks.

It is equally important to acknowledge the contribution of experts and researchers who have developed our knowledge of the helping process. I cannot thank certain theorists enough. So my work with students has always been a passionate struggle to promote theory and put it into practice, so that we are not just working by intuition or experience, important though these are. This book therefore references some of the foundations on which my own work is built. I hope that it takes the essence of theory and helps to apply it, so that I share my experience with yours. To these ends each chapter has a small exercise which 'grounds' the theory. Some are my own versions of standard exercises, others are original. They are all well tested and simple to use – on your own or with others.

Within this book, I have attempted to select some of the most important issues which have emerged through my own practice and experience. It is intended to develop first the practitioner's *awareness*, then *knowledge*.

I have consciously placed an emphasis on practice issues. Knowledge of related law and policy is clearly important, and these are areas that change regularly – you need to back up the material in this book by consulting your employer's documents, and other reliable sources.

In writing about work with reluctant clients, this book does effectively re-examine many social work customs and conventions, because clients who do not want services need you to be especially flexible and sensitive. The adage is: take people and issues seriously, but not yourself!

CONTENT

The first part of the book is about things which would be helpful to think about before making contact with a client. Then, some important issues which commonly arise in an encounter with a reluctant client are highlighted. As they all overlap, you can 'dip and sip' if you like.

I am a white, able-bodied, heterosexual woman, and inevitably the book obviously does reflect my own personal perspective. Throughout the workbook I will try to highlight areas where it is particularly important to recognise that other perspectives may be different from the ones which people often take for granted, particularly in matters of age, disability, class, race, gender and sexuality. I have where possible included a broad range of perspectives within the book, and apologise if the reader finds any of the content in this book insensitive or inaccurate – I would love to hear from anyone who would like a dialogue with me.

Some of the topics in the book apply to working with people generally, not just involuntary clients. If a few of these seem obvious, ask yourself why they are not taken seriously more often!

SOME DEFINITIONS

Many words used in textbooks and ordinary life are confusing because they are either misunderstood altogether, or mean different things to different people. Therefore, below I provide some definitions of a few important words which communicate the way in which they will be used in the book.

Culture
'An identity which everyone has, based on a number of factors such as: memories, ethnic background, family attitudes to child rearing, class, money, religious or other celebrations, division of family roles according to gender or age' (Bernard and Baderin 2002, p.21).

Discrimination
When someone is treated less favourably than other people are/ would be treated; discrimination applies even if the negative impact is unintentional.

Black and minority ethnic
This denotes any minority group who have a shared race, nationality or language and culture. This definition includes Eastern Europeans and Travellers, Black African and Black Caribbean people, Asian

and East Asian people and people who are mixed race, all of whom can experience prejudice based on their shared characteristics.

Heterosexual
Someone who is attracted to persons of the opposite sex, emotionally and/or physically.

Lesbian
A woman who is attracted to other women, emotionally and/or physically.

Bisexual
Someone who is attracted to both sexes, emotionally and/or physically.

Gay man
A man who is emotionally and/or physically attracted to other men. The term 'gay' is also commonly used to describe any homosexual, whether man or woman.

Disabled person
Someone who has a physical or mental impairment that has a substantial and long-term adverse effect on his or her ability to carry out normal day-to-day activities (Disability Discrimination Act 1995).

Transgender and trans
Broad terms that refer to people who live part or all of their lives in their preferred gender role. This includes people who may cross-dress or undergo some hormone treatment, but not necessarily full gender reassignment, as well as transsexual people (Commission for Social Care Inspection 2008).

Gender
The behaviour, activities and attributes that a given society considers appropriate for men and women. Aspects of sex will not vary

substantially between different human societies, while aspects of gender may vary greatly (World Health Organization 2008).

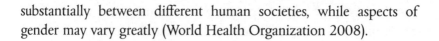

Exercise: Your personal starting point

You may have come by this book in all sorts of ways. Take a moment to reflect on what you hope to gain from using it, and write down a small list. This deceptively simple exercise will be important later.

My personal starting point

To end the beginnings, I wish to acknowledge that my interest in reluctant clients springs as much from my own fierce independence and sense of inadequacy as a human being, as from any grand principle. I do not find it difficult to understand why people do bad things, or refuse to accept help.

Summary

- Clients who have not chosen to be service users are the most challenging, and therefore the most rewarding to work with.
- Reluctant clients are usually people who are defined by *others* to be in some sort of need. There is a spectrum of reluctance.
- Practitioners and clients are not 'friends' to anyone whom we are helping in a professional context – blurring the distinction between friendship and this other kind of help usually leads to misunderstanding, and can do actual harm.
- It's important to be aware of your own personal perspective and appreciate that others will have different perspectives.
- Clients who do not want services need you to be especially flexible and sensitive.

2. Your Philosophy

What you believe matters…

…maybe more than you think.

BELIEF AND HOW IT RELATES TO PRACTICE

At the start of this chapter, it makes sense to first describe what I mean by the term 'belief' – I am primarily talking about an individual's beliefs about life and people. This may include your moral and ethical views, whether or not you subscribe to a religion.

As helpers we would all agree that our ability to feel for people or feel with people – empathy – is very important. Those of us involved in caring work do our best to give a good service, whatever our own personal views, which we keep to ourselves.

In this way, those in the helping professions are expected to keep their professional and private lives separate; most workplace codes of practice expect this. If you work for a faith-based or politically based organisation, you may feel it is an advantage to have ideals in common with colleagues and clients, and to able to express these.

Whichever applies, I wonder if we always operate exactly as we think we are; in other words, are we influenced by background and the society we are in far more than we imagine? It is important not to be complacent about this, and worth looking a little more closely at beliefs which may be quite unconscious.

UNCONSCIOUS BELIEFS AND VALUES

In order to try to avoid the following discussion being rather nebulous in an otherwise practical book, I list below some examples of 'results' which link directly to underlying beliefs.

For example, Trotter (1990) studied the kinds of relationships probation officers built with their charges, and found that when such officers had a sympathetic outlook and made frequent comments which seemed to excuse the crimes that their clients committed, such as 'I can quite understand why you stole the money to buy drugs' – which the offender might take as condoning the offence – re-offending rates tended to increase.

Trotter then developed an approach which emphasised offering praise and reward for behaviour which was in keeping with a desire to avoid offending, for example not mixing with other offenders, and seeking work (Trotter 1996). Clients were not encouraged to make any kinds of excuses for their behaviour, whatever the worker's own feelings. Trotter trained 12 probation officers in the approach and followed up 104 of their clients. He compared the outcomes for this experimental group with outcomes for a control group of 157 probation clients. Clients in the experimental group were subsequently significantly more likely to report that their problems were reduced and their re-offence rates were also significantly lower than those in the control group.

The above denotes a subtle importance in the use of workers' feelings. Where anti-social behaviour is concerned, we may have to go against our instincts to express warmth and empathy. Of course, the basic values of respect, consistency and courtesy underline this approach; indeed they are vital, as the worker is a model for the client – what Trotter calls 'pro-social modelling'.

Perhaps this revelation is something of a relief, as there will certainly be people you cannot empathise with: murderers and child abusers being examples for many people.

On the other hand, several researchers have strengthened my own personal conviction that, if the helper believes that the client can change for the better, this is more likely to happen. This could also be described as optimism. The book *Learned Optimism: How to Change Your Mind and Your Life* by Martin Seligman (1995) has almost become a classic in education as an accessible book that is based in research. Within the book, Seligman describes the way young people 'catch' the mental attitude of the teacher.

More recently, Miller and Rollnick (2004) studied interviews between workers and clients in depth as part of their book, *Motivational Interviewing* (an approach which describes how to work through client ambivalence to facilitate change). In the book, they highlight the important part worker optimism plays in achieving change.

It's worth bearing in mind that clients can usually sense the true feelings of a worker – a point backed up by Chris Trotter's study, 'Probation can work: A research study using volunteers' (1990). He noted that, when probation officers made negative comments about clients such as 'lazy' or 'no-hoper' in their file notes, their clients had a higher re-offending rate. It is as if words like 'lazy' and 'manipulative' come over the airwaves from your office to your client as surely as if you had shouted them through a loudspeaker. These descriptions then translate themselves into attitudes – beliefs become reality.

TAKING CONTROL OF YOUR BELIEFS

So, we cannot help our feelings, but how can we get past them to become a more effective helper of people – even those whose behaviour may arouse in us nothing but disgust?

First, it may not be possible to control your thoughts, but it is possible to control your actions. This might be consciously preventing your dislike of someone from translating into your punishing them. This is easier said than done, and it can be a great help to have someone trustworthy to talk to about such situations.

Second, you can be tactfully honest; if someone is not allowing you to get a word in, or is insidiously making sexual overtures, it is much better to say, 'It is difficult to go on while…', or whatever form of words is comfortable for you, than to let the situation run on. Again, it is hard to put this into practice, especially with someone who has not actually asked for you. A personal example which springs to mind: a client asked me to negotiate with the Benefits Agency for her – I refused to do so until she had stopped giving the Agency false information.

Even though you may have to keep some thoughts to yourself, the key issue is to understand behaviour. The act of understanding particular kinds of behaviour can put them in a whole new light. An example of this might be a person in a hospital who hurts themselves, and in doing so generates anger from staff who don't understand why they have done it but do have to treat them, blocking beds for people who, in their view, 'really deserve them'. The act of hurting yourself is often called 'deliberate self-harm', and even this expression introduces the idea of blame on a very unhappy person in need of help.

The Royal College of Psychiatrists says that self-harm can help you to feel in control, and reduce uncomfortable feelings of tension and distress (2007). If you feel guilty, it can be a way of punishing yourself and relieving your guilt. Either way, it can become a 'quick fix' for feeling bad. I have heard so many young people put this clinical description in their own words: 'It makes me feel better,' or 'When I cut myself, the pain takes away the pain inside.'

So, when working with a reluctant client, bear the above in mind. Before you meet the client, take the time to reflect a little: What is it about this client which makes you feel scared, irritated or helpless?

It is unlikely to be just their actions – usually it is much more subtle things which throw us off course – their voice, expression or the state of their home. Having identified something off-putting, instead of the instinctive tendency we have to try to ignore it, and *stay with it.*

For example, when meeting the client who intimidates by moving too close to you, and invades your personal space, think about how this makes you feel. Which parts of your body are involved – which are not? Staying with your discomfort in this way can cause it to change. You may feel tired and feel like relaxing for a few minutes, or you may feel renewed energy. Once you give your body and mind this kind of close attention, you can feel differently about someone or something. This may be why pretending to be happy can actually have real physical effects. The above strategies are derived from McDermott and O'Connor (1996). Food for thought!

CONSCIOUS BELIEFS

What about the place of more conscious and specific beliefs which you or the clients may hold? Clearly, professional neutrality dictates that health and social care workers need to be able to respond appropriately to the needs of all service users, including those who might hold very different religious, spiritual or moral beliefs from your own.

To help clients actively to practise their religion, you may need assistance from a colleague or advocate if you lack the necessary understanding of the faith which they embrace. Confinement and solitary living is a reality for many involuntary clients, and those who are isolated can sometimes find strength and solace in religion.

In a British study undertaken between 2003 and 2004 (Gilligan 2006), social work students were found to be less likely than their qualified colleagues to consider religious or spiritually sensitive kinds of practice, reflecting the largely secular society in the UK. Interestingly, attitudes varied little between those students who held religious beliefs and those who did not. However, there is increasing awareness of the importance of acknowledging spirituality and religion as practitioners in health and social care are increasingly being encouraged to embrace a more holistic way of thinking about clients – not as patients to be 'cured', but as individuals with their own values, attitudes and beliefs who can become involved in the services they receive; we all have to find meaning and a sense of belonging.

Religious congregations may offer support where family and community do not. It is also interesting that within the mental health field researchers have found clinical evidence to support the positive influence of religion in people's lives, specifically:

- fewer hospitalization days

- fewer days in jail or prison

- more days in school

- more days on the job

- fewer suicides

- less spouse, child and elderly abuse.

(Ben Asher 2001, p.4)

In the same piece of work, Ben Asher goes on to highlight some of the concerns people might have about the role of belief and religion in social work (p.5):

> One of our greatest concerns about making religion and spirituality an integral part of social work is the possibility that some practitioners will impose their beliefs on the people with whom they are working, both beneficiaries and colleagues. One can imagine a triumphalism in which a social worker acts as if he or she has been exclusively entrusted with insight into the divine will.

But Ben Asher concludes that:

> Such assertions, ironically, do not necessarily reflect belief in a higher power, often they are based on a belief in one's own power, that one can manipulate God for one's personal purposes.

The concern a person has about someone's religious belief could equally apply to any strongly held beliefs or principles you have – political, secularist or pacifist. They will always be a base for your practice, but this does not mean that you have to disclose them to your client – I personally would always err on the side of extreme caution unless there is a very good reason for disclosure.

Exercise: My beliefs and actions

This exercise is about your beliefs – it is not a knowledge test. You can do it on your own, or in a group. Answer 'yes', 'no' or 'it depends' depending on whether you agree with the following statements:

1. People need to take risks to learn how to manage risks.

2. A woman prisoner should not be allowed to have a baby.

3. I agree with the practice of circumcision.

4. It is OK for some religions to prohibit same-sex relationships.

5. Having faith helps mentally ill people to get better.

6. When the client accepts the service which has been imposed on him or her, there is a better chance of success.

7. I do not think this book will change my basic beliefs.

8. It is important to find out the truth about things, and challenge clients who lie.

9. Compelling people to accept treatment does not really work, except to protect others.

10. Most parents who abuse their children are reluctant to accept help.

Discussion

Consider your responses to the above statements. If most of your responses were 'it depends', is this because you are a very analytical person, or because you find it difficult to commit yourself to an opinion? If you had mostly 'yes' or 'no' you have firm beliefs – where do they come from? Your parents, your church, your social group...? You may be interested in relevant research findings and recommended practice in relation to the statements.

People need to take risks to learn how to manage risks

In protective services such as residential care homes, approaches to risk have in the past been concerned with avoiding potentially harmful situations to service users and staff. However, the law actually requires that clients experience some level of risk taking to enable them to develop the necessary skills associated with ordinary living; this is known as elective risk. This is in order to strike a balance between the health and safety of the individual and their independence, which should not be unnecessarily curtailed (Health and Safety Executive 2000).

A woman prisoner should not be allowed to have a baby

Prisoners can apply to start a family with their partner by use of artificial insemination. Prison department policy is that this should only be allowed where there are exceptionally strong reasons, and where the applicant couple are legally married. Article 12 of the European Convention on Human Rights Convention guarantees the right to marry and found a family, so a refusal by the Prison Department to allow a prisoner to marry or to start a family by artificial insemination could be challenged under this article (Liberty 2008).

I agree with the practice of circumcision

Sometimes circumcision has to be carried out for medical reasons. This may be because the foreskin is damaged or infected and will not slide back over the head of the penis. Only around one in every 100 men need a circumcision for medical reasons, but in the UK the number of circumcisions carried out is roughly six times higher than this. Female circumcision is illegal in the UK. Circumcision is often carried out for religious reasons. For example, in religions such as Judaism and Islam, it is an important ritual. Some cultures practise circumcision for hygiene reasons, and see the foreskin as unnecessary, or as causing health problems. Many people have strong views about whether or not circumcision should be carried out. It is not routinely performed in the UK because there is no clear clinical evidence to suggest that it has any medical benefit (National Health Service Institute for Innovation and Improvement undated).

It is OK for some religions to prohibit same-sex relationships

A survey of six focus groups with people who are Christian, Muslim, Jewish and Hindu and lesbian and gay people within those faith communities carried out by Ruth Hunt and Gill Valentine and entitled *Love Thy Neighbour: What People of Faith Really Think about Homosexuality* (Hunt and Valentine 2008) found that some parts of faith communities objected to lesbian and gay sexuality, but that these objections were often over-emphasised, and narrowly reflected by both religious leaders on the one hand and by the media on the other. They suggested that younger people of faith were more likely to think about their faith, rather than be concerned about attitudes to others.

Having faith helps mentally ill people to get better

Research carried out by the Royal College of Psychiatrists has found that, in healthcare, spirituality is identified with experiencing a deep-seated sense of meaning and purpose in life, together with a sense of belonging. It is about acceptance, integration and wholeness. Patients have identified the following benefits of faith:

- Improved self-control, self-esteem and confidence.

- Faster and easier recovery, achieved through both promoting the healthy grieving of loss and maximising personal potential.

- Improved relationships – with self and others and with God/creation/ nature.

- A new sense of meaning, resulting in reawakening of hope and peace of mind, enabling people to accept and live with problems not yet resolved.

(Royal College of Psychiatrists 2006, p.3)

When the client accepts the service which has been imposed on him or her, there is a better chance of success

This may well be true in a lot of cases, but it is not always certain – some research has shown that clients who are eager to please can feel just as angry and resistant as the less accepting ones, and are consenting in order to protect themselves (Rooney 1992).

I do not think this book will change my basic beliefs

A book probably won't! Good practice can only be 'caught' from others. You will recognise from your own experience in school, college or workplace how much the whole atmosphere is affected for good or ill by the people in charge. In a research review on the teaching of communication in social work education, Diggins writes that:

> what...emerges is the view that values and principles cannot be taught, only learnt, and that this learning takes place best where it is modelled in the culture of the department and setting within which students learn, and specifically through supervision and tutorials where that learning is drawn out and made explicit. (Diggins 2004, p.28)

It is important to find out the truth about things, and challenge clients who lie

On the face of it, this sounds like something that most people would agree with, but remember that there may be a very good reason why the client is lying. Lying and deception are basic survival strategies and are often used by individuals who struggle to obtain access to valued resources (DePaulo *et al.* 1996).

Compelling people to accept treatment does not really work, except to protect others

In Britain, studies in the mental health field reported that compulsion helped patients maintain contact with health professionals and also that patients agreed to accept medication (Atkinson *et al.* 2002). Other experts have noted that our expectations of involuntary clients are much lower (Marlowe *et al.* 2001). This may prejudice the results much more than the fact of compulsion, if our underlying attitudes really do count as much as I think they do.

Most parents who abuse their children are reluctant to accept help

At face value, this statement appears to be true. However, outright denials of need for assistance or help from helping practitioners and angry rebuffs are more often about communicating the way a parent feels they have been treated rather than communicating the intervention they actually need. My experience is that it takes a long time for the truth about abuse to emerge, if it ever does. 'I love my kids' may be as near as you will get to a request for your help – it is certainly a starting point. In my experience and that of others working in this area, parents feel mistrustful and unheard by professionals, but most nevertheless acknowledge that they need help, even if this is not expressed directly (Yatchmenoff 2008).

· ·

I hope that you have found some food for thought in the above. My intention is to encourage you to challenge your own beliefs and to be a 'critical practitioner' – willing to think about your own practice in relation to legal frameworks and research.

CONCLUSION

As with all personal work, there are no cast-iron recipes for effective practice, but my experience is that increased understanding of both yourself and the client can make dramatic changes.

This is a complicated matter, as becoming more understanding is not something you can always do at will. Your inability to understand some aspects of others may be deeply embedded in your own background, or you may simply lack some of the essential life experiences or experiences of pain which you can draw on when working with clients in new or uncomfortable situations.

However, I believe that negotiating new or uncomfortable experiences *can* to some extent be learned, and indeed that it is often necessary to experience a degree of discomfort in order to become more empathic.

The clients who teach you the most are the ones whom you find hardest; this commonly includes involuntary clients who have committed actions you find difficult to forgive. Obviously your own specific situation at the time plays a part. For example, if you are a survivor of recent domestic violence you can hardly be expected to trust that your client's abusing behaviour is going to change. It is also helpful at times to avoid certain situations at certain times in your life: for example bereavement counsellors usually advise the recently bereaved not to work with people in the same situation for a few months.

When working with reluctant clients, it's important to take care of yourself as well as to take care of them – having someone trustworthy to talk to is absolutely essential.

Summary

- Beliefs, whether religious or personal, unconscious or conscious, form an essential part of ourselves and our clients.
- It's important to be aware of your own beliefs in order to work with your client effectively and impartially.
- Take care to ensure that your sympathy for clients' situations does not translate into unhelpful practice.
- Be tactfully honest.
- Above all, make an effort to *understand* your client.
- Make sure you take care of yourself and seek the advice and counsel of a colleague when dealing with a client who you find difficult to work with.

FURTHER INFORMATION

Husain, F. (2005) *Cultural Competence in Family Support: A Toolkit for Working with Black, Minority Ethnic and Faith Families.* London: National Family and Parenting Institute.

This toolkit offers sections on a variety of issues of importance for family support, such as culture, discrimination, family and communication. In addition, detailed religious fact sheets are available on Buddhism, Christianity, Hinduism, Islam, Judaism, Rastafarianism and Sikhism.

3. Helping Others

She spent her life helping others...

...you could tell the others by the hunted look.

HUNTING AND HELPING

The above quotation is from the late C.S. Lewis (2001, p.10) – a wise and sensitive observer of human beings. It is certainly the case that those working with involuntary clients do have to engage in 'hunting' of a kind. The 'helping' side of the work is much more complicated.

It can be very hard to remember that, sometimes, genuine help can involve avoiding finding solutions for people, at least until some rapport has been established. For example, it may be tempting to arrive for the first session with a briefcase full of leaflets about exciting services. In some circumstances this may be absolutely appropriate, but when people have not asked for your help, you could be seen as another doorstep salesperson whom they can't wait to get rid of!

The nature of our particular work is that we are expected to find solutions for people who do not want our services, but have no choice but to receive them.

So, whose solutions are they? Very often, they are general rules and guidelines which are consistent with the standards shared within our wider society, but are not always helpful to the individual person concerned in a particular case. For example, older frail people are often placed into care in a safe environment. This may be positive for some older people, but for others, the experience can lead them to simply give up and die. It is worth looking a little more closely at the nature of 'helping'.

My approach in this book is that there are all kinds of health and social carers, not all of them professional. In thinking of the much maligned word 'professional' many people's minds jump to 'being paid'. However, the dictionary definition gives a more useful clue: 'professionalism relates to work which needs special education or training' (Cambridge Online Dictionary 2010).

I believe passionately in the importance of training for work which, whether paid or not, gives us huge amounts of power over clients. Training actually increases our power, hence the saying 'knowledge is power' – this is a necessary evil. Take a deceptively simple task such as taking a client you do not know very well on a visit. If you are a professional, or trained helper, you may not perform better, but you should have the potential to see the implications of the outing, and relate it to the client's total life, much more clearly.

For example, during the visit the client might well express feeling about not being able to cope. It would very easy to respond to this by offering residential care, day care, home carers, sheltered housing and many other constructive ideas. However, this would very definitely be jumping to solutions. In order to use our knowledge power really well, it is useful to understand why we wish to find solutions for situations – this is not as obvious as it seems! So we need to understand something of our own motivation – a vital aspect of skilled helping which next claims our attention.

MOTIVATIONS FOR HELPING

Social psychologists have suggested that people's motives for helping others are not as clear as we might think. For example, some forms of caring, such as protecting our children, promote survival and thereby help to perpetuate our genes. Self-interest is a powerful motivator for us – we enjoy the thanks and possible praise from the boss or colleagues, or simply the pleasure of making something better. There is nothing wrong with any of this, so long as we are clear that we are 'helping' ourselves (Hogg and Vaughan 2005, p.64).

Sometimes people are motivated by feeling pain at the distress of clients – the act of helping the client to avoid your own pain means that whether or not that person wants your help becomes irrelevant. People are more likely to lend a hand when someone appears both to need and *deserve* assistance – this is often not the case when working with involuntary clients, but the helping practitioners can still enjoy the challenge of supporting a client to overcome their initial resistance to receive help.

The foregoing may have given the impression that it is somehow wrong to admit to less than altruistic motives. I remember being disconcerted when one mentor, whom I respected very much, commented that social work was 'a positive indulgence' for me. I now believe that it does not much matter *why* we are helping, as long as we *know* why we are doing so.

STARTING THE HELPING WORK

Approaching with the right attitude

When starting work with an involuntary client, it pays to be cautious. You may initially think that you have to do much more than is necessary – take care not to give the impression that *everything* you are suggesting is compulsory.

The role of helper requires that clients accept us, and will trust us not to 'force feed' them. For some clients, however, treatment programmes are non-negotiable, such as those for paedophilia. If compulsory measures make it possible for clients to remain in the community, and keep members of the public safe, they are certainly justified, I believe. The law has the power to impose such *provisions* –

prison being a prime example – but not the *services* which accompany these. I recall a visiting clergyman being somewhat annoyed that one of his parishioners, who was behind bars, had the right to refuse to see him. We can deprive someone of his or her liberty, but 'helping' is another matter.

Another common mistake is to try to help a client by offering them inappropriate reassurance. I remember my first experience of introducing a client to a care home. The welcoming staff member said to him: 'Don't worry, all your problems are over now, we will feed you, clothe you and look after you.' The client must have heard the door of the condemned cell clanging behind him – every shred of independence being taken away!

Even where the client is there of his or her own volition, research suggests reassurance is a limited tool (Hamilton and Dinat 2006). Hamilton and Dinat say reassurance seems like a helping technique, but can be the opposite, namely an attempt by the professional to avoid the pain which the client is facing. For example, when we are very anxious, it doesn't help for a well-meaning professional to say 'It will be all right', even when this happens to be an accurate statement. My experience is, however, that reassurance can be an important ingredient of crisis counselling, because it is a part of information giving, which is so vital in circumstances when we feel out of control. For example, in the case of delayed travel, the fact that people are often left by the authorities with no information weighs far heavier than the delay itself.

Problems can arise if you act according to your own personality type rather than respond to someone else's. Isabel Briggs Myers and her mother, Katharine Briggs, developed a personality inventory called the Myers–Briggs Type Indicator which was based on Jung's theory of psychological types and is widely used today in all kinds of ways. Two of the most relevant types for us as helpers are described in her book with Peter B. Myers, *Gifts Differing* (1995). She says that 'perceivers' – people who like to be open to everyone and everything, do not make judgements about people until they have to, and do not like to say 'no' to people – are possibly flexible and spontaneous at work when responding to unforeseen circumstances. The other type noted by the Myers–Briggs Type Indicator are the 'judgers', who like to know where they are with people, make decisions quickly, and want to find solutions. Such behaviour could lead to a tendency to rush into providing things for clients before they are ready. When these two types work together, there can be clashes: the perceiver finding the judger far too hasty and rule-bound, whereas the judger cannot stand the tardiness of the perceiver's decision making. If both types understand their differences, and value them, they progress to seeing how much they rely on each other. Judgers often make excellent assessors where quick thinking is essential, but situations also need helpers to stand back and re-evaluate. It is therefore interesting that the 'do as you would be done by' principle has to be modified somewhat in skilled helping.

For a very readable, in-depth discussion of the Myers–Briggs Type Indicator and its implications for teamwork, see the 'Further information' section at the end of the chapter.

ADAPTING YOUR APPROACH TO COMMUNICATION FOR DIFFERENT CLIENTS

There are some aspects of communication which are particularly important for helping reluctant clients.

For example, when two people of different cultures are trying to work together, they may perceive one another as unfriendly. They are not aware that they are operating according to different sets of rules for certain topics. For example, someone who grew up in Saudi Arabia with Arabic values is more likely to be curious to know about your marital status, number of children (or the reason for not having any) and salary than someone holding typically Western values, who might consider such questions personal. The person from Saudi Arabia may therefore not pick up on the other person's reluctance to discuss such matters, particularly if there are language barriers (Genera and Kharrat 2000).

At a very basic level, being able to understand each other's language is key to working with reluctant clients effectively. The use of interpreters is often where reluctant clients who do not speak English need most help.

The following guidance comes from the Race Equality in Practice Resource Pack, Department of Health, Social Services and Public Safety, Northern Ireland (2003), and is valid for all types of interpretation:

> It is important to use professional, trained, interpreters. If there is a personal relationship between patient and interpreter, as in the case of family members providing this service, impartiality and client confidentiality may be compromised.
>
> The 'interpreter' may withhold important information – for example, a woman who is depressed because of her marriage may not be able to get to the root of the trouble if her husband is acting as interpreter. Since the patient is known to him/her, the 'interpreter' may report what they think they ought to say, rather than what was actually said.
>
> Some professionals claim that interpreters are not necessary since they can access someone on their own staff who speaks the relevant language. However, although this is preferable to using friends or relatives, it is generally not good practice, except in emergency situations, since these members of staff were employed to do a particular job, not to act as interpreters. (Department of Health, Social Services and Public Safety, Northern Ireland 2003, pp.24–25)

All staff should therefore have guidelines on how to deal with translation and interpretation.

Remember, what you may perceive as reluctance on the part of the client may be normal behaviour for them, and your own actions can inadvertently create barriers to communication. For some, it is difficult to talk about things which are personal or intimate. For some Asian clients this may be magnified as revelations of personal or social problems may reflect not only on the individual, but also on the whole family in a culture where family reputation is very important (Robinson 2004).

Breaking off eye contact with a deaf person when he or she is giving information is rude and will increasingly irritate him or her, leading to shorter and shorter replies. Even when the person gives more information than can be remembered, it is better not to break eye contact in order to write it down. One possibility is to sign/

explain on the need to write, but the likelihood is that this will affect the flow of the interview (Centre for Deaf Studies 2009).

Being 'force fed', sometimes literally and frequently metaphorically, is the daily experience of a large proportion of clients with a physical disability, who have no choice about receiving services. In recent years groups for people with disability have tried to educate the more able-bodied of us out of our insensitive, well-meaning ways of 'help' by all sorts of awareness-raising activities. If you do not have a disability yourself, it is impossible to understand how it feels to be dependent on others in everyday life, so it is essential to receive training from those who really know, either as clients or as carers. This is the philosophy behind People First, an organisation made up of people with learning disabilities and their support workers, who provide training for organisations and individuals who need it.

. . . .

Exercise: Practice!

Here are some everyday situations. Respond to each as though you are the person concerned.

1. You are being interviewed for a job.
    One of the interview panel members is a wheelchair user. The panel chairperson asks you to move the person in the wheelchair across the room.

    I would...

2. You are attending a team meeting.
    The item under discussion is what can be done to encourage people with disabilities to apply for a carer's post which has become vacant. The team works with clients who themselves have disabilities, and often need practical services such as helping with personal care and toileting.

    I think...

3. You are working in a hostel for young disabled people.
    The philosophy of the establishment is self-direction at all times. You are asked by a young male client to put his woollens in the washer on the hot programme, thereby ruining them.

    I would...

4. You work at a residential school.

    You are asked at the last moment to take Melanie, a 14-year-old girl who is a wheelchair user, and who weighs 15 stone, on a field trip. You have the requisite number of helpers for the number of pupils, but Melanie would need a support worker for herself at all times. You know that educational visits are included in the 'education and associated services' as defined in the Special Educational Needs and Disability Act 2001, so a school must not discriminate against a disabled pupil in relation to any educational visits which the school plans or undertakes.

    I would...

Follow-up

1. What did you do or say?

    This is a real situation where the applicant should ask the panel member if and how he or she wished to be moved. The unwary applicant would 'help out' without asking – I imagine he or she was unsuccessful! Judith Usiskin (1998), whose expertise derives directly from clients, says that a good rule of thumb is to ask the person what they want or need you to do.

2. There is not a definite answer to this one – rather some further questions:

    Did you express any reservations about employing a disabled person in a situation where a lot of physical work is involved? If not, was it because you were afraid of being 'politically incorrect'? If you did, what do you imagine the response to be from other team members?

    What was your mental picture of a disabled person? Did you automatically assume they would need a lot of support?

    Did you consider what might need to be done before you could recruit someone with a disability: adaptation to the building, support worker, mentor?

    The moral of this one is: think about the assumptions you and others may be making about 'a disabled person'. He or she may need minimal physical support, since disability covers everything from mental health problems to learning difficulties.

3. How did you respond: did you comply with the request and ruin the clothes, or did you suggest a cool wash would be better?

This was a real situation experienced by a student carer. I admit I would have been tempted to put the washer on a more appropriate setting. The challenge is to offer choice to people first, in this case by pointing out the different wash cycles, before taking action on their behalf – an example of the kind of ordinary experience able-bodied people take for granted: to learn by trial and error. The guiding principle of the hostel where the above incident took place was that helping others means doing only that which clients cannot do themselves – acting as their arms and legs, but not their central nervous system. It sounds so obvious when you think about it.

'The foundation of genuine helping lies in being ordinary' (Brandon 1982, p.8). David Brandon was quite remarkable for being a pioneer in taking social work theory and practice away from being a sort of adapted psychotherapy, and for challenging some of what he saw as its inhuman 'professionalism'. You may be interested to know more about him – see reference in the 'Further information' section below.

4. Would you take Melanie on the outing?

    You are keen to help, so as not to discriminate, but are worried about the practical aspects. Realistically, the question hinges on whether there is enough available support for you. If not, it would be unsafe to take her. The staff team needs to do some work on not raising a young person's hopes before doing adequate planning.

    Finally, how far were your responses based on your personal experience of disability?

· ·

We are rightly constantly challenged by people who are forced to receive services. We cannot ever be adequate in meeting need, as the following real-life example demonstrates.

A worker had just finished what he thought was a very thorough assessment of a client's needs, including a range of services, medical help and home care. The worker's supervisor spoke to the client to check the assessment, and asked him what he thought his needs were. The client replied, 'Some sex, some legs and a car.'

Summary

- We have to hunt down involuntary clients, but helping them is a much more complex matter.
- It pays to look closely into your motives for helping people, and for whose benefit you are working.
- Don't overface new clients with too much information when you first meet them.
- If you offer reassurance, make sure it's appropriate.
- Be sensitive to the cultural sensitivities of the client.
- Adapt your approach to communication to meet the needs of the individual client.
- Remember to put the client at the centre of your work – to listen to them and to ask them about what they want.

FURTHER INFORMATION

Goldsmith, M. and Kindred, M. (2001) *Developing Teamwork...From an Understanding of Personality.* Southwell: 4M Publications.

Smith, M. (2006) *David Brandon: Homelessness, Advocacy and Zen in the Art of Helping.* London: Infed. Accessed on 19/05/10 at www.infed.org/thinkers/david_brandon_zen_helping.htm

    This article examines David Brandon's contribution to our understanding of the experience of homelessness and mental health problems, and his insights into the nature of advocacy and the helping process.

Usiskin, J. (1998) *Working with Disability.* Ely: Fenman.

4. Messages

Sending messages...

...not the ones you thought, though.

FIRST IMPRESSIONS

'Messages' has been placed before non-verbal communication, although the two are closely related. Both are about what begins to happen even before you speak.

When we meet someone, a large number of impressions take root in each of us faster than the speed of light, and certainly before we have said hello.

An example would be the fleeting thoughts you may have when you see what kind of car a visitor has just parked outside your house. A student once described the whole of my lifestyle on the basis that I drove a Ford Fiesta! Making a judgement about someone's smart or otherwise car is possibly easily recognised, but there are dozens of small but significant decisions which we all make about another person and we may not even be aware of doing so. These judgements or 'assumptions' (probably a better word) can change the whole way a relationship goes, because they bring with them a small, unseen label which says bad or good.

Your reluctant client has almost certainly had negative experiences with professionals, so all your efforts to be friendly and present yourself helpfully are played against this background, even if the client greets you politely. You can take for granted, I believe, that a huge number of negative assumptions are being made about you, and that these will not be easily shifted. It helps to be comfortable with this, and not to try to prove yourself – which can only be done over time and may happen only partially. Be prepared for never coming over as the concerned, honest person you really are.

Now – test this out!

. . . .

Exercise: Assumptions

You need either to do this one with a small group of colleagues whom you don't know well, or a group of friends who can be relied on to be honest. People you don't know come closer to replicating a meeting with a new client, but also expect some surprises from people who know you well. You will need a big piece of paper and felt pen. It would be helpful for a group member to agree to write notes on the paper for you.

1. Explain to the group that you are going to ask them to make guesses about things they don't know about you, using facts they do know. These need to be things you can answer yes or no to, not guesses about your feelings or personal qualities, as these can vary from day to day, or may be subjective. Example: 'I think you are teetotal since I've never seen you drink alcohol.'

2. Ask your helper to write each example on the piece of paper but don't give the answers until everyone has finished guessing.

3. Now give an honest yes or no to each guess.

4. Next comes the risky bit: ask the contributor of each statement what their guess, or assumption, about you made them feel towards you. Example: 'When I said I thought you were a teetotaller, in my heart of hearts I think teetotallers are a bit goody-goody' – a negative impression, revealing the contributor's personal attitude to alcohol.

5. Discuss the accuracy or otherwise of people's assumptions, and the sort of evidence they had for them.

Comment

I am willing to bet that there were a few surprises all round. We are always finding out things about people, even if we make a career of it!

· ·

IMPLICATIONS

Remember, first impressions are powerful – and physical appearance has a strong influence. A group of dentists, Leishman, Bisset and Walkden (2005), found that gender and age as well as facial expression were the most significant factors in influencing choice of practitioner. They commented (p.21):

> Obviously we cannot do anything regarding our gender or age, so must make a conscious effort to maintain a pleasant and happy expression when meeting and dealing with our patients!

Food for thought!

People often assume that others have inner qualities that correspond to their observable behaviour, but this isn't always the case – it is worth devoting extra thought before you form a firm impression. Research by Smith and Mackie (2007), into initial assessments by social workers, confirmed that one might be particularly motivated to form accurate assessments of people when having to work with them, or when being suspicious about someone's ulterior motives. Relying on a single characteristic relies on past judgements and evaluations, rather than the underlying evidence, for example someone appears to be open and honest when we first meet them, so we do not examine their statements too closely.

It's equally important to avoid making judgements based on physical environments and accessories – like my Ford Fiesta!

In supervision settings, social workers will often present a biased case by choosing what information to mention to their supervisor and how to present it.

This is not usually because of any conscious intention to mislead the supervisor but because facts and interpretations that fit their existing beliefs will come to mind more readily and more vividly than details that cast doubt on them.

It is as if they have unconsciously chosen to act either for the defence or the prosecution of the client (Munro 1995). We do not easily change our mind and tend to pay most attention to information that endorses our belief while overlooking evidence that challenges it. In statutory work, this common feature of reasoning can seriously bias and distort assessment. Smith and Mackie (2007) found that in courtrooms such distortions persist even after information is found to be false.

So there is a need to examine our assumptions. What can we do about them? The example below is specific to social work, but the principles are equally applicable to other helping professionals.

MOVING ON

> The first step is to be clear about what the social worker's first judgement actually is. The supervisor needs to encourage social workers to say what their 'general feeling' or 'gut reaction' was to the client. If for instance they are investigating a child abuse allegation which the parents deny, is their initial feeling after speaking to the parents that the accusation may be true or do the parents seem quite caring and honest so that they are inclined to believe their explanation of events? (Munro 1995, p.6)

We are looking to make ourselves more accurate when forming opinions – Smith and Mackie (2007) say that it is only when people are actively looking for change in themselves or others that this actually happens.

Munro (1995) suggests that the most effective way to reduce the effects of our impressions is explicitly to consider an opposite possibility.

> Testing judgements requires social workers to acknowledge the possibility of being wrong, and to make a deliberate effort to look for and consider the evidence against their initial appraisal.
> (Munro 1995, p.8)

This is a challenging thought, especially if we feel very positive about someone on first meeting.

All the authorities say that getting to know someone well helps, but is not the whole answer to correcting bias, as you will have found if you did the exercise with close friends or colleagues.

Finally, one further important point is made by Smith and Mackie which highlights the importance of the approach of the person working with the reluctant client:

> Initial impressions of someone create corresponding behaviours towards this person. The other person can act in ways to meet with the expectations. This is called the self-fulfilling prophecy.
> (Smith and Mackie 2007, p.60)

So, though we have to do the utmost to correct our bias, if we send out a positive and hopeful message when we begin working with a client, then he or she is more likely to live up to it. When people are actively looking for change in an individual, fundamental change is possible.

Summary

- Our first, often unconscious, impressions of people are very important.
- We can change some things about the way we present ourselves, and some things we can't.

- We need to examine our first impressions, and the conclusions we draw from them, with others who may have a different view.
- Scrutinising the evidence for our impressions is essential.
- Where sound evidence points us to change our judgements, we have to be willing to do so.
- First impressions can actually influence outcomes.
- If we are actively looking for change in people, this is more likely to happen.

FURTHER INFORMATION

Archer, D. (1991): *A World of Gestures*. Berkeley, CA: Berkeley Media. Accessed on 19/05/10 at www.berkeleymedia.com/catalog.

5. Power

You may feel yourself to be up against formidable opposition...

...it is worth remembering that the other person may feel exactly the same.

THE NATURE OF POWER

Put yourself in the position of someone who is new to the art of trying to help someone in a professional or caring way. It is normal to feel very nervous, and that you do not have a lot of control.

In fact, one of the paradoxes of the act of helping a reluctant client is that forcing the client to accept help immediately places the client in a powerless position – in your own life, you may have experienced a comparable feeling when in the dentist's chair, or on the operating table. However, if someone has been ordered to have assistance, or has a disability which gives them no choice, this feeling of powerlessness is magnified a thousand times.

So, for the practitioner who is new to helping, there can be feelings of helplessness on both sides. It is a challenging thought to consider that we are part of our client's problem – and we can often be told as much in no uncertain terms! Accepting this unpalatable fact, and letting the other person know that you have done so, is a big step towards establishing rapport.

When considering power and relationships, it's worth remembering that it is not power in itself which is wrong: we need the dentist's knowledge-based power, and an abused child needs professional power to do something to help. I believe that even involuntary service users accept this kind of power, in their heart of hearts. Research with clients says:

> it is the arbitrary and inappropriate use of such powers, without adequate information or warning which service users have long expressed most concern about. The existence of such powers does not in itself inherently exclude the possibility of service users being involved and having a say in what happens to them. But they do report concerns that this does not always happen and that safeguards are inadequate. (Beresford 2007, p.46)

Some experts would go as far as to tell us that the work of social workers and other helping professionals is fundamentally about the use of various kinds of power – even if the thought of this might be uncomfortable to you (Webb 2000).

THE ABUSE OF POWER

Given that we like to see ourselves as caring, respectful and ethical, why is there so much bad practice – is it all 'other people'? Unfortunately research is not on our side here, so it is worth looking at some of our own behaviour a bit more critically.

Focusing on social workers, Webb (2000) found that, though practitioners may try to produce change in their clients, they also often try to preserve their own status and methods of working, and thereby resist change themselves.

Perhaps you recognise something like the following in your own or others' dealings with people: 'My training tells me that this child is not developing normally for her age,' or 'You need to let Nila be more independent.' Though these assertions may be true or well founded, such examples of communicating advice are not likely to achieve a warm or cooperative relationship with clients. They may *frighten* parents or carers into changing their ways, and thus we may feel we have been successful in this use of power. However, to speak this way to a client is to contravene some of the basic touchstones of good practice, such as showing sensitivity to the client, their problems and their circumstances.

Even when we are doing our best to be friendly and positive about situations, we can get it horribly wrong. I can remember vividly being in a client's house where the electricity had been cut off. She had put candles all round the walls, and the room looked lovely. Without thinking first, I said so. Instantaneously, I saw her face fall, and how patronising I had been. Being in the dark because you cannot pay the electricity bill is *not* the same as putting up Christmas decorations in a warm and comfortable home. The difference is about the power imbalance:

> A social worker is party to personal information that can make for an unequal footing. If you said to somebody, 'you look smart' or 'that is a nice coat' – that would be OK. But to say, 'you look lovely' is too much of a comment on what you look like. If I was a social worker I would be careful about saying that to a client. (Client, in Parker 2009, p.24)

GOOD AND BAD LABELS

Nobody likes being labelled, and in my experience professionals, carers and parents shy away from them. However, some labels are actually helpful, others are less so, but essential, and the rest are plain horrible. I should like to comment first on the helpful ones.

When they are ill, most people feel more comfortable if the doctor can tell them what is wrong. It is true that we fear the frightening illnesses, and therefore their names, and so doctors used to be reluctant to tell people their diagnosis – this was especially true in the case of mental illness. Recently people have begun to expect more openness, plus the amount of information on the web has meant that people make their own diagnoses – with varying degrees of accuracy, it has to be said!

I remember protecting my clients from frightening labels, for example the mother of a child who was to be sent to a 'maladjusted school'. When the mother found out the nature of the boarding school, she was understandably furious that I had not been straight with her. It would have been much better to find respectful words to describe the kind of service her son needed, and to help her to accept it, which I had to do anyway, having impeded myself by setting up a barrier.

Recently I have experienced very good examples of practice, where some of the most mentally ill and dangerous people in society had been given their diagnoses, and at every step the implications of their illness and treatments were discussed. In the end this communicates respect to the patient.

The next positive use of labels is that of a 'passport' to obtain services or benefits. A good example of this is people who have 'personality disorders', a vague term which used to mean that those classified as having a personality disorder received no treatment. Now, there has been useful work on this condition, for example Hill, who says:

> One of the problems with all kinds of personality disorder is the perception that the people concerned can change themselves if they really wish to do so and that it is therefore their fault if they do not. We therefore tend to blame people who have a personality disorder. Yet is it right to assume that people can change through sheer effort of will? (2007, p.1)

Hill goes on to outline the kinds of treatment which work for this condition, the principles of which are to make people aware of what they do to others, why they do it and then to give them the support that allows them to behave differently. Crucially this group of people are now defined as 'mentally ill' for the purposes of receiving benefits or services.

POWER IN RELATIONSHIPS WITH COLLEAGUES

We are all aware of aspects of this – the relationship between your boss and yourself being an obvious example. However, there are some more subtle power relationships within the workplace which are also worth examining in order to make your work with clients clearer. In quite ordinary situations, people who appear to have power arc not always the ones you might think. To illustrate this, try the following:

. . . .

Exercise: The power tree*

---

*   Substantially reproduced, by permission, from Kindred and Kindred (2001) *Once Upon a Team Exercises* © 4M Publications.

You can do this one as an individual, or as a work group, in which case you need to draw out the tree on a large piece of paper, and have a felt tip pen handy.

NB This is a deceptively simple exercise, which can bring out strong feelings in a work group. Make sure you have plenty of time for discussion.

Individual version

1. Think of your family, a group of people with whom you work, or a club to which you belong.

2. Draw yourself somewhere on the power tree to show how you feel in relation to other people in the family or group, the top part of the tree being the most powerful.

3. Draw the others in the group where you feel they are in relation to you and each other. This may or may not be related to your position in the family or group, e.g. you could be the eldest in the family or the manager of a team, yet feel yourself to be right at the bottom of the 'pecking order'.

Group version

1. Everyone draws themselves somewhere on the power tree to show how they feel in relation to other people in the team, the top part of the tree being the most powerful.

Discussion

Did you discover any surprises? If so, it may be helpful to start by revisiting the fact that all groups, from the highest-powered corporation to the most informal of organisations in a small village, depend on the use of power. It is sometimes said that people who want power have the potential to use it well. This is a dangerous generalisation, but we can all think of people who have had power thrust upon them, perhaps for career reasons or for financial gain, who have struggled and who have wished that they had not achieved it. If this applies, remember that you have got the potential to develop.

Looking again at your power tree, was the boss automatically placed at the top, and the administrative staff at the bottom? How often have you heard someone saying they are 'just the receptionist'. It may be helpful here to make a distinction between influence which you can have whatever your role, and power, which is bestowed on you by your role, e.g. parents, bosses and leaders all have power. Children, employees and group members can and do have a very strong influence. Use or misuse of power and influence applies to everyone. The person who is low-paid but has the key for a particular cupboard is very influential, and has it within his or her grasp to stop productivity for a day – this makes him or her as important as the boss for a time. It is the labels which accompany the power which make people squirm: 'I'm only the secretary.' 'He's a manipulator.'

Involuntary clients have no power so long as they are clients, however strong their *influence* may seem when they are refusing to do something you need them to do. Also, someone can have considerable power at work, but if they happen to be black or have a visible disability, they will still be disempowered in the street – such is the nature of prejudice.

> I sometimes think that 99 per cent of suffering has to do with how devalued people feel by the labels put on them or the derogatory opinions they hold about themselves. (Hoffman 1993, p.79)

. . . .

If we are surprised, and perhaps a little disconcerted, at the hidden agendas and less-than-obvious power relationships between colleagues, how much more important it is that we look again at our work with involuntary clients. We know that such clients do not have a choice about working with us, but are we sure they are always given their legitimate rights, for example to refuse certain services? In the end, we have the lion's share of power, but this does not equal therapy.

Summary

- It is important to recognise how much power we have as workers.
- We often abuse our power without meaning to.
- Labelling people can be helpful in ensuring that they actually get some help, though labels are also destructive.
- The use of power by different individuals in organisations is not as obvious as you may think.

FURTHER INFORMATION

Kindred, M. and Kindred, M. (2001) *Once Upon a Group Exercises.* Southwell: 4M Publications.

6. Non-verbal Communication

Something we know about…

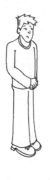

…perhaps needs further examination.

WHY EXAMINE IT?

It is easy to ignore the effects of non-verbal communication, even though we know it exists, often because we often do not know how it is exhibited! It is worth being aware of in your own work because involuntary clients will be far less forgiving than polite social contacts.

Imagine a scenario where you are mis-communicating: you do not know what you are saying, and your client is put off by what you do say. It is hard to imagine a situation where you really have no idea of what you are saying, but this can reflect reality when we 'speak' non-verbally. Awareness of our non-verbal communication is particularly important when we are communicating with people whose racial or cultural backgrounds are different from our own. It's useful to draw on the findings of researchers here, as we cannot hope to have an accurate picture outside our own experience.

HOW WE COMMUNICATE NON-VERBALLY

Facial expression

Argyle (1996, p.121) writes about six basic emotions that are communicated through facial expression: happiness, surprise, fear, sadness, anger and disgust/contempt. Do you think you would be able to recognise these? It is likely you would, since they are largely thought to be universal and so recognisable by people from most cultures. However, Argyle highlights that we sometimes find it difficult to control facial expression.

Writing in relation to hospital and social care settings, Williams (1997, p.12) also writes that we need to guard our facial messages carefully: 'professionals working in a healthcare context need to monitor their facial expressions to prevent them communicating feelings of disgust or revulsion'. For instance, if you are treating a messy wound, you may communicate disgust. How much more so when you are faced not only with messy wounds, but behaviour you find unacceptable.

Eye contact or gaze

It really is important to know a little about how people from different races and cultures differ in the way in which they use body language to interact and communicate.

To take the example of the use of eyes with one particular group, Lena Robinson (2004, p.117), a well-respected practice teacher and researcher, says, 'eye contact during verbal communication is expected in Western culture because it implies attention and respect toward others. Among Asians, eye contact is considered a sign of lack of respect and attention, particularly to authority and older people.'

We use eye contact to signal threat, intimacy and interest. It is also used to regulate turn-taking in conversation and is a key factor in deciding how interested the listener is in what we are saying. Listeners usually make eye contact for about 70–75 per cent of the time, with each gaze averaging 7.8 seconds, according to Argyle (1996). We may need to modify this according to the client we are working with; on the one hand ensuring we communicate interest, recognition and support, but not threatening Asian people by overdoing our length of gaze.

In group work settings, Finlay (2001) reminds us that it is particularly important to include all members of a group in face-to-face contact:

> This is a skill that requires practice, but it is crucial if we want to communicate interest, recognition and support for all group members. Moreover, we can use our eye contact effectively to encourage one person to speak and to discourage others. (Finlay 2001, p.43)

One very important point for working with reluctant clients: I have noticed that when I am putting people under pressure by asking difficult questions, they will often close their eyes, look up at the sky, or look away. This is not evasiveness – it is a natural response to discomfort.

Gesture

The use of gesture is probably one of the most culture-specific forms of non-verbal communication, and can lead to misinterpretations and accidental insults. For example, the act of holding out an arm and making a circle with thumb and forefinger together – used by the French and sometimes the British to indicate something is perfect – would be considered vulgar by someone living in the Mediterranean region, as it would be thought to denote the vagina (Axtell 1998).

Gestures of particular significance to the health professional are those described as 'self-touching actions', such as touching the face, scratching, gripping the hands together or putting the hands in or near the mouth, because they can be signs of tension or stress (Rowe 2006). When working with involuntary clients, all signs of stress are particularly important: blushing, perspiring, changes in breathing, flushing, muscle tension, moisture in eyes, blanching, flaring of nostrils, unconscious movement of body parts, visceral experience, numbing, and temperature changes (Blatner 2002). Also these signs often occur when people are experiencing intense emotions such as depression, elation or extreme anxiety.

I once failed with a young man by not noticing how stressed he was when I mentioned his family at the beginning of our contact – the relationship never really recovered.

Posture

As long ago as the 1980s, Michael Argyle (1988), a pioneer in the study of non-verbal communication as related to the helping professions, pinpointed the importance of sitting in an attentive pose, leaning forward very slightly, without crossing the legs. Though it is very difficult to remember posture as well as all the other things, just making ourselves aware of the significance of our way of sitting in the chair, and how clients may respond, in itself tends to change our behaviour.

Touch

I think there was a time when the subject of touch received very little attention in caring circles. Parents and carers gave comfort as came naturally within their own culture. It has also been documented that people of higher status or power touch those of lesser status significantly more frequently than the converse (Hunter and Struve 1998).

Sexual abuse happened, but was not talked about in as open a way as it is today, though carers, doctors and therapists would perhaps have been given guidelines during the course of their training. In the last 20 years, abuse has been recognised as a much more prevalent problem than most people thought. This has led to extremely strict guidelines being given to all professionals, and advice being given to parents and relatives about how to be more aware of the issues. They are now encouraged to be thoughtful about their use of physical contact within the family.

When I was working with residential staff in a young persons' unit, the most worrying issue of all for the male workers was being accused of sexual malconduct. Some carers and teachers now avoid using physical contact to comfort children and young people. So where do you stand on this issue?

If you work for an organisation, it is likely to have definite rules. You may not agree with all of them, but they should be clear and you need to act in accordance with them. If you are an informal carer, or do not have guidelines in your organisation, you may find it more difficult to judge how to act – is an intuitive response as a human being the same as a professional response? You may feel uneasy about what you should or should not be doing.

I certainly recognise this from my own working life in recent years. A look at the experience and expertise of therapists is instructive. Reminder: this book is written within European/American culture and using experts from this culture. You will need to adapt and find out what is acceptable in other cultures, though this will take a lifetime!

In this book, touch is defined as hand-holding, having your arm around someone's shoulders, touching an arm and, in the case of small children, cuddling. The latter is sometimes used by psychotherapists with adults, though this may not be allowed because of the prevalence of abuse. You need to consult your workplace policy if you are employed, and use extreme discretion if you are a volunteer.

Consider the specific situations below.

1. THE BEREAVED PERSON

This is a situation where comfort in the form of touch can be most helpful, according to Tschudin (1997). More than comfort, touching someone actually assists in the bereaved person gathering strength. However, there is no consensus. Trotter (2006) recently reviewed the literature, and found that there are many different views. My advice, therefore, can only be ambivalent: if you are confident, go ahead and use touch in this context – if in doubt, don't!

2. MEMORY AND TOUCH

If you work with someone whose memory has been lost, either temporarily or permanently, you will probably have already discovered the importance of physical contact to put someone in touch with experiences they cannot describe in words. For example, if someone has lost contact with the world as you experience it, through dementia, your gentle hand-holding can remind them of the relationships they had, and so provide comfort. A word of warning: if someone has been physically or sexually abused they may react negatively to all touching. Development of trust to the point of this being overcome will then be a wonderful breakthrough.

3. HELPING SOMEONE TO CONFIDE

I have found that, if you touch someone sensitively at the right time for them, this helps in trust formation. If this seems obvious, it is worth noting that the timing is absolutely crucial, and that there are no guidelines as to when. You will no doubt remember the times when someone got it wrong for you!

Some experts say that we cannot thrive as infants without being touched (Field 1995). This may be a theory that is difficult to prove or disprove, but it is worth remembering that many of us have been short of good touching during our lifetime. Your caring gestures toward those you look after may therefore be a lot more important than you think. I hope that some training, plus your own intuition, will help you to feel safe with this very human aspect of skilled helping.

Space

Most people know that it is not helpful to invade another person's personal space by getting too close to them. Wainwright (2003, p.68) summarises acceptable distances as follows:

- 0 to 1.5 feet (0–0.5m) is the intimate zone, in which people can easily touch each other.

- 1.5 to 4 feet (0.5–1.2m) is the personal zone, in which people are able to shake hands.

- 4 to 10 feet (1.2–3m) is the social consultative zone, which is most commonly used in everyday social or business encounters.

- 10 feet and over (3m plus) is the public zone.

There is a tension here: you need to avoid appearing defensive, so try not to sit behind a desk, on a higher chair than your client or stand when he or she is sitting – anything which could enhance your powerful position. Avoiding being defensive is not the same as being unsafe – it is trying to leave as much control in the hands of your client as you possibly can. A biologist friend of mine once pointed out that we are much nearer the animal kingdom than we like to think. Perhaps that is why our territory is so important to us – *don't* sit in the boss's chair!

Don't forget the messages of the physical environment:

> Research in psychology is now showing that the colors of walls, carpets and furniture and the layout of a room can affect our mood, feelings and how we behave. To this end psychotherapists are being consulted about the decoration of prison cells for violent prisoners. The effect of this is to try and curb violent behavior and graffiti. A senior probation officer recently told me that he had put into interviewing rooms (which had suffered badly from vandalism) quality furniture and decorations and that in six months there had been no damage done. (Webb 2000, p.1)

Finally, here is some *conscious* non-verbal communication to remember Signed language or non-verbal communication techniques are something that non-hearing people already do really well. If we all took more time trying to learn or harness these skills the workplace would be a much more pleasant and equal space in which those with hearing difficulties could thrive and be active members of the team. Similarly people without sight do not need nearly as much 'support' as you might think. I have personal experience of a non-sighted receptionist who could lead me and others with ease around a workplace which resembled an abondoned warehouse, then do everything which was expected administratively.

. . . .

Exercise: Test your own non-verbal communication

You need to enlist the help of a partner during a staff meeting. Explain that all he or she has to do is to make a note of the non-verbal signals he or she picks up from you during the meeting. You will let the other group members know that you are trying to improve your skills in non-verbal communication, but that you are not in any way assessing them, nor is the person making notes; he or she will only be observing you. In practice they will probably all be so intrigued that they will start observing each other!

During the meeting, communicate the following messages non-verbally to your partner, using as many of the types of non-verbal means as you can. Do not overact so as not to spoil the meeting and to make the exercise as natural as possible. Do one every five minutes, spending about 30 seconds on each.

Messages to communicate:

1. Why doesn't the person next to you shut up so that you can hear what's going on in the meeting?

2. You agree with the point just made by A, who is sitting across the table.

3. Your rushed lunch doesn't agree with your stomach.

4. You want to say something if there is time left.

5. You want very strongly to answer the person who just spoke, but you keep getting interrupted.

6. You want a stick of gum which someone else has in their pocket.

7. You're tired and you want to go home.

(Adapted from Center for Rural Studies 1998)

Afterwards

You will expect to hear from your partner after the meeting, unless everyone is so curious that they want to hear what your partner has recorded now. If so, check that your partner is happy to do this, as it is important that he or she does not feel that he or she is being tested. Wherever it takes place, it will be an interesting discussion, including all sorts of messages which were not on your agenda!

Finally, spare some thoughts about your own identity. How did your behaviour reflect your:

- racial background?
- social class background?

- gender?

- state of physical ability or disability?

- sexual orientation?

- age?

· ·

Even if you do not know the answer to this question, the exercise will have made you much more acute in watching others from different worlds, picking up clues as you go.

So why learn to observe by doing? The reason is that you feel yourself into different situations which are not so different from what happens naturally when you are not thinking about them – the principle behind acting and role playing.

We learn, I believe, not from texts or other resources, but from someone. (Al-Mahmood and McLoughlin 2004, p.6)

Summary

- We need to examine our non-verbal communication because it speaks louder than our words.

- Being conscious of our facial expression, eye contact, gesture, posture, touch and use of space is particularly relevant in a multi-cultural context.

- There are conscious kinds of non-verbal communication, and certain groups are experts in using these.

- It is important to develop skills in reading other people's non-verbal communication.

FURTHER INFORMATION

Borg, J. (2008) *Body Language: 7 Easy Lessons to Master the Silent Language.* Up Saddle River, NJ: Prentice Hall.

Hogan, K. (2009) *Body Language: The Basics.* Eagan, MN: Network 3000 Publishing. Accessed on 19/05/10 at www.kevinhogan.com/nonverbal-communication-body-language.htm.

7. Dress

How you look does matter...

...for whom are you dressing?

DRESSING FOR THE CLIENT

Many people would say that we have to dress for our clients. This might appear to be one of the world's obvious statements, but it needs unpicking.

I am a conventional-looking older woman – should I try to make myself look like a teenager in order to establish rapport with a teenager? If we were to take this road it would be difficult to see how anyone would make a connection with the diverse range of individuals they encounter within the space of a day. On the other hand, it is important to make your choice of clothes appropriate to your professional role rather than your leisure time.

Wearing conspicuously expensive-looking clothes is unlikely to endear you to a poor person. On the other hand, 'dressing down' could be seen as patronising and insulting. Formal occasions such as court require you to discard your more casual wear if you are to attain the best result for your client. Both men and women need to think about whether their clothes are sexually provocative. It is notable that psychotherapists have told me many times that their experience has led them to furnish both their persons and their rooms in a warm, welcoming but non-controversial way.

In a practice setting, individuality is best expressed through your responses to people rather than through your dress – the points I have been making about your facial expression and attitude are much more important.

DRESS CODES

Organisations say that they expect you to 'dress in a professional manner'. In recent years this vague statement has been expanded by most employers into a detailed code of practice.

In order to meet the requirements of safety and anti-discriminatory practice, employers must consider the reasons behind each part of their dress codes. For example, within the National Health Service (NHS) specific clothing is required for health and safety or hygiene reasons.

It is necessary for employers to consult with employees and their representatives and unions, particularly if there are a significant number of employees of a particular religion who may be affected by a dress code. Equally they need to be sensitive in the approach to the enforcement of a code. If an individual feels that an employer is trying to compromise their religious beliefs by enforcing a dress code it can be upsetting for that employee – a heavy-handed approach is likely to exacerbate this. Finally, they must be consistent in their approach. It would be very difficult to justify a dress code in a tribunal if that code is otherwise widely flouted by other employees with the employer's tacit consent (National Health Service 2007).

Even so, employers find it difficult to avoid discrimination:

> [A] Muslim healthcare professional left her agency post at the Royal Berkshire Hospital Trust in Reading, claiming she had been forced out because she refused to bare her arms. According to Islamic law, a woman should cover her arms, including the wrist, at all times except in front of close relatives. (Mooney 2008, p.1)

Note: all the above is for discussion purposes. If you are employed you must consult your agency dress code.

Obviously the above rules apply to all settings, but if clients are involuntary they may be more affected by staff dress codes, particularly if no one has explained the reasons for them.

DRESS CODES FOR CLIENTS

Dilemmas about discrimination and safety do not end with workers:

> A 45-year-old man with learning disabilities has recently started wearing women's clothing at the day centre and in the local town. He is becoming alienated from his peers at the day centre by cross-dressing. He is also being targeted by local youths. If he continues to wear women's clothing he risks being victimised. In spite of initial reluctance from his parents, a compromise is reached where he is permitted to wear women's clothing in the safe environment of the family home. (Drinkwater 2009)

This solution could give the impression to service users that 'difference' is something that should be discouraged. However, if there were a cross-dresser on the staff of the centre, an excellent role model would be provided.

What do you think? One professional body has some interesting views:

> Dress codes may be much more relaxed in informal practice settings such as mental health, but choice of colour may be significant. A former psychiatric patient comments how frightened he was, when in a paranoid state, of nurses dressed in black clothes. Studies of patient preferences in a UK complementary medicine

clinic showed older patients favoured more formal white uniforms. These findings mirror those from similar studies in Israel and the USA. (Chartered Society of Physiotherapists 2009, p.3)

Now a bit of fun with a serious purpose!

• •

Exercise: Making dress choices

You can do this one yourself, but it is much better with a group of friends or colleagues.

1. As a group, each of you in turn explain how you chose the clothes you are wearing today.

2. In the responses, note how far people have consciously dressed:

    (a) to please the people they are going to meet

    (b) to please themselves

    (c) to suit the activities they are going on to after the group they are in now.

3. Note the differences between men and women on this topic.

4. Debrief by reading and discussing the following:

    Many people approach this exercise in a straightforward manner: citing 'comfort', 'what I could find' or 'the weather'.

    Observers have noted other common characteristics. Check the following with your group:

    •   Are you sending a message? We all do this unconsciously, but for some it is important to do so intentionally, such as the transgendered person who wishes to be as anonymous as possible, the gay person who would like to let other gay people know their orientation, or the straight person who wishes to attract the opposite sex.

    •   You may dress with personal safety in mind: for example certain kinds of earrings and necklaces can catch on equipment, or be pulled by violent people.

    •   If you like to wear body-revealing clothing, it is worth noting that Abbey et al. (1987) found that members of both sexes were perceived as kind and warm when wearing non-revealing clothing. Al-Sayyad and Adams (2006) say that clothes express everyone's sexual orientation, whatever this may be. Presumably there is a subtle language which one needs to learn.

- You may wish to make a religious statement by what you wear – there has been much controversy about this in recent years. Does your workplace have a policy about the wearing of religious symbols?

- If you have to wear a uniform, are you happy about this? One large firm in the UK issues a similar uniform to everyone from top management to the most junior and this is found to be a great social leveller, not least because employees' clothes budgets can be spent on leisure clothes!

- Finally, as a group, see if you can come to any conclusions which affect the way you each dress tomorrow.

- Obviously it is not within the spirit of this book for judgemental comments to be made about other people's apparel. Rather, it is interesting to notice points coming up which you or others may not have thought about.

. . . .

I am very well aware that you may disagree with aspects of the above. In 40 years of experience I have never known a group of professionals reach complete agreement on a dress code! However, there does seem to be some accord on the starting principle: dress for your client, not for you.

Summary

- There is a general consensus that we should dress for our clients, but this is not as simple as it seems.
- Dress codes are common in organisations, but there are points for and against.
- The way we dress has an impact on the impression we give to others and on their reaction to us.

- Sometimes, there can be a tension between your responsibility to help the client and the client's rights to dress as they wish.
- We do not always put our opinions about how to dress appropriately into everyday practice.

FURTHER INFORMATION

National Health Service (2007) *Dress Codes and Discrimination.* London: NHS. Accessed on 19/05/10 at www.nhsemployers.org/EmploymentPolicyAndPractice/EqualityAndDiversity/Pages/DressCodesAndDiscrimination.aspx.

8. Rights

Have I any rights at all...

...if so, what are they?

RIGHTS AND NEEDS

The idea that people have rights, even in relation to their own well-being, goes back long before social care textbooks. For example, the philosopher John Stuart Mill wrote in 1869 that:

> the only purpose for which power can be rightfully exercised over any member of a civilised community, against his will, is to prevent harm to others. His own good, either physical or moral, is not a sufficient warrant. (Mill and Gray 2008, p.8)

However, in care settings we veer intuitively to try to help the person as well as keeping them from harm.

Involuntary clients often have a very strong sense of being deprived of their rights. You may feel that some of them have brought this on themselves, and that others are simply unfortunate in being forced to accept help through no fault of their own. All have equal cause to feel aggrieved at your invasion of their lives. It is therefore worth taking a look at different kinds of 'taking over', with a view to making the process as constructive as possible.

THE LEGAL POSITION

Helping people when they don't want you to is in fact a very complicated matter, and the law has evolved to ensure we keep within strict guidelines, which become ever more involved with the need to accord with national, European and international legal frameworks.

First there is the Human Rights legislation, defined in 1948 in the Universal Declaration of Human Rights, and the Human Rights Act 1998, 'intended to place human rights at the heart of public service delivery, and through this to make rights a reality for all people in the UK' (Department of Health 2007, p.36).

One of the most important principles of the Human Rights Act for involuntary clients and their carers is the right to control one's own destiny.

English law assumes that, if you're an adult, you are able to make your own decisions, unless it's proven otherwise. As long as you can understand and weigh up the information you need to make the decision, you should be able to make it. If you are suffering from a serious mental illness, it may be necessary for you to stay in hospital under the Mental Health Act 1983. If so, you may be given treatment for your mental disorder, even if you do not consent. However, the terms of that Act only apply to treatment for mental disorder. You may also have a physical disorder that has nothing to do with your mental condition. If treatment is suggested for that, you are entitled to choose whether or not to accept it, as long as you are able to understand enough about the choices to make a decision (Department of Health 2001).

The Mental Capacity Act 2005 contains the law that applies to anyone who lacks the mental capacity needed to make some or all of their own decisions. In certain circumstances, the Act allows a decision to be taken by one person on behalf of another.

For example, a Local Authority may appoint an Advocate to support a person who lacks capacity but has no one to speak for them, such as family or friends. The Advocate makes representations about the person's wishes, feelings, beliefs and values, at the same time as bringing to the attention of the decision-maker all factors that are relevant to the decision.

It also allows individuals to plan ahead for a time when they might lose the capacity for decision making. A person's capacity may be permanently affected, for example, by a form of dementia, or for a temporary period because of a short illness (Mind 2009).

If someone wishes to kill themselves, our society says this is not a crime (Suicide Act 1961), whatever your personal view. The strength of organisations such as the Samaritans is in their leaving the client free to make even such an extreme choice, though of course they use every possible resource to try to help the client find life-preserving paths.

Readers of this book are likely to be practitioners who are face to face with their clients due to the requirements of law or extreme need, and who have a duty to decide whether someone is a danger to him or herself or others, then to remove that danger, albeit temporarily.

The law is changing all the time, and the above only sets out some of the basic principles. You need to supplement these with more detailed guidance by referring to the 'Further information' section at the end of the chapter.

INFRINGEMENT OF RIGHTS

Below are some examples of cases in which clients' rights are infringed:

- A consultant encountered an older woman on a hospital ward in London, who was crying out in distress. It became apparent that the woman was upset at having been strapped into her wheelchair by the nursing staff. The nurses explained that they had not wanted her to walk around in light of her high risk of falling and sustaining an injury. Whilst understanding their concerns, the consultant suggested their actions were inappropriate and could be considered degrading. She was unstrapped and subsequent physiotherapy improved her mobility.

- A couple with learning disabilities who live in residential care homes were prevented from marrying.

- Unreasonable restrictions being placed on family visits in hospitals and residential care homes.

- People with dementia in hospitals as informal patients being told that the exit is somewhere else in order to prevent them from leaving.

    (Age Concern and British Institute of Human Rights 2009)

Can you think of examples from your own experience?

Most infringements stem from concern and anxiety about risk, though it has to be said that inadequate staffing levels are sometimes to blame. Whatever the cause we are not doing involuntary clients any favours by overprotecting them:

> Quite simply we cannot hope to improve people's health and well-being if we are not ensuring that their human rights are respected. Human rights are not just about avoiding getting it wrong, they are an opportunity to make real improvements to people's lives.
> (Social Care Institute for Excellence 2008, p.1)

CARE AND RIGHTS

In spite of all the conditions, all clients, including reluctant ones, have a substantial number of rights, however extreme their situation, though it is not usually helpful to point this out. The beginnings of a list from the National Occupational Standards for Social Work

(TOPSS 2004, pp.4–5), which also cover all social care, might go something like this. Your client has the right to:

- be treated with respect regardless of age, ethnicity, culture, level of understanding, and need

- have honest information about the power invested in social carers, including legal powers

- be informed about when information needs to be shared with others

- be consulted about decisions affecting them

- be supported in challenging discriminatory images and practices affecting themselves or their families

- have respect for his or her private and family life.

The Human Rights Act 2008 has made the latter a particular tenet, which is significant for involuntary clients because they often depend on us to maintain and forge links with their sometimes estranged families.

Your client does not have the right to:

- abuse you verbally in any way at all, but especially on grounds of race, gender, sexual orientation, age, disability or social standing

- be violent towards you

- threaten or subject you to emotional pressure.

Verbal abuse is a difficult area, and it would be hard to find a consensus about it. I began my career by thinking that clients needed to shout at me, and that letting them do so was a helpful release. Over the years I have come to the position that allowing people to abuse me verbally actually demeans them – they can do without this as they are so demeaned already. So you may agree with me that it is useful to tell the person gently that you do not like what they have just said, or that you won't accept it. Exceptions: if someone is out of touch with reality, either through illness, alcohol or drugs, there is no point in challenging, and it may even be dangerous to do so.

Threatening to withdraw the service is always wrong in the context of involuntary clients, because it is not an option. Perhaps, though, it is right to change the worker if, for example, abuse is based on someone's colour or gender. This also has its negative side, as a change to a white worker from a black one may be seen as colluding with racism. On complex matters such as these the worker's rights to be consulted about such decisions certainly come into the foreground.

Now some practice!

. . . .

Exercise: Dilemma for helper and client

1. Imagine you go by appointment to visit Alice, an 80-year-old woman whom you know quite well. She is not particularly frail, but has recently been in hospital for a routine operation, and you were called in to provide some support on her return home, because she had once had a blackout. She is extremely independent, and has asked you to leave her alone on several occasions. However, she is always polite and opens the door to you.

2. When you reach Alice's house, you ring the bell, but there is no answer. You look through the window and see that she is sitting in her usual chair, asleep. However, she is slumped in an uncomfortable-looking position, almost on the floor. You knock on the window, but fail to rouse her. You go away for half an hour and return. Alice is in exactly the same position, and again does not respond to your knocking.

3. You have three alternatives:
   - return later today
   - return another day
   - call the police to see whether forced entry is appropriate.

   Which do you choose?

I found that this situation aroused strong feelings when offered to students in training. It goes to the heart of the human rights versus duty of care debate. Whichever way you choose to proceed, you would obviously not do so without consultation. During this process you may find the arguments reproduced between senior personnel, the police if you decide to involve them, and friends/colleagues. If you are asked to proceed in a way which seems to you inhuman, such as leaving a situation alone when you think it needs action, it is worth just asking whether you may need saving from yourself. Situations which definitely need prompt action are in one sense the easy ones. 'Alice' could land you before a complaints panel if you invade her home and she objects, or a coroner's court if you decide to leave her and she dies.

• •

Most people would agree that depriving someone of their liberty or privacy is a disagreeable thing to do. However, experience tells me that some clients are very clear that they are not quite strong enough to look after themselves completely. So my guiding principle, which may be different from yours: better to have someone alive and angry than dead but unviolated.

Summary

- There is a complex relationship between rights and needs.
- The current legal position on human rights leaves many gaps.
- We are therefore faced with dilemmas, and rights are sometimes infringed.
- Workers in the caring services have rights too and they should not tolerate abuse.

FURTHER INFORMATION

Department of Constitutional Affairs (2006) *A Guide to the Human Rights Act 1998*. London: Department of Constitutional Affairs.

9. Staying Safe

Personal safety...

...a topic which needs some attention.

STARTING POINT

> Deeds of violence in our society are performed largely by those trying to establish their self-esteem, to defend their self-image, and to demonstrate that they, too, are significant. (May 1972, p.21)

Many involuntary clients are thus described, so the need for personal safety must be faced squarely. I wish to strike a balance between over-emphasising danger and pretending that some clients do not have the potential for harm.

IMPORTANT PROVISOS

This chapter is not Health and Safety training; it shares some thoughts which have been drawn from both my own experience and that of others. Where guidelines are offered, they must always be used in conjunction with your workplace policies, never as a substitute for them. We actually have a duty:

- to keep ourselves safe

- to share information about people with a history of previous problems or aggressive behaviour with colleagues or other agencies as appropriate

- to notify our line managers of potentially high-risk situations in order to gain appropriate support in dealing with possible difficulties.

It is very important that you do not see reporting as a failure on your part.

WORKING WITH PEOPLE IN A SAFE WAY

My experience and reading tell me that there are quite significant things we can do to keep ourselves safer. These can be summed up as techniques which may partially or wholly reduce the person's hostility.

Quite simply this is about communication, over which we all have some degree of control, and which can be improved through training.

If you make home visits, remember that, whereas you may view the visit as an explicit demonstration of a desire to help, the client may perceive it as threatening. If in any doubt about your contact, take someone with you.

Whatever the venue, when you meet your client it is vital to ask how the person sees things *now*. What they tell you will give you some pointers as to how far or near they seem from other people's perceptions of them. It is usually impossible to negotiate with someone drunk or drugged. If you suspect any life-threatening behaviour or condition, get help quickly. If in any doubt during your contact, leave if you are scared, and keep well out of arm's reach.

Then there is your response to cues: I remember being taught how important it is to respond quickly when acting in a play, otherwise the scene goes completely flat. In skilled helping your response needs to be so fast at times as to be instantaneous, when anticipating someone's mood or illness level.

Knowing that the same cue has different meanings according to your cultural roots is really crucial here. For example, as a British woman I was brought up to understand that 'not looking someone in the eye' is either devious or rude. My female contemporaries, whose family roots may be in Eastern cultures, may well lower their eyes out of modesty or deference, particularly if they are speaking to a man.

Triggers for violence may be quite simple, for example being too hot or cold, being excited about an activity or event or feeling disappointed about something. It is obvious that the environment matters: harsh lighting, high noise levels or being nearby when someone else has an outburst may all be triggers. You may notice stress symptoms such as increased perspiration or difficulty in concentration.

My experience is that horror and violent films definitely affect some people with mental health problems, because the latter have high sensitivity. This is worth considering if you are watching television with your client.

Reluctant clients often come with a history of negative experiences of authority. However hard you and others are trying, they may feel that they are being ignored, made fun of, publicly humiliated or treated in a disrespectful or condescending manner. Being singled out, wrongly accused, victimised, 'bossed about' or the subject of racial or homophobic prejudice are everyday realities. In addition clients may be distressed about the withdrawal of, or being deprived of, a service they feel is essential.

To counteract this: Is it possible for us to make a homelike and helpful workplace? Making a home from home means loosening the routine to something like that of a real household – and it might even be easier to run. Also, if it feels more like home, it might encourage people to talk to and support each other more easily instead of entering into confrontation.

And there is the so simple matter of giving people time. The provision of protected times for staff to speak with clients has been shown to lead to improvements in communication and a positive difference to client attitudes (Age Concern 2007).

Being honest does not make you into another negative authority figure. I have found clients value statements such as, 'I find you scary when you speak to me like that,' or 'I really can't take you in my car if you won't wear a seat belt.' The latter has its perils – I once found a client had been pretending to wear his belt over many miles of motoring in order to please me. He had a phobia about being trapped, and had solved the problem in his own way. Such are the hazards of 'people' work!

BEFORE MAKING ANY CONTACT WITH A CLIENT

You do need to know if the person you are going to meet has any history of violence. Some people, particularly informal carers, do not like to know about someone's past, as they do not wish to form judgements. It may be useful to unpick this a little: while it is quite true that clients often feel they have been pre-judged, many are reassured by your awareness of how they have come to be in their current position. It can be much more embarrassing and difficult, even tedious, to have to tell the whole story again to someone. You can only decide about whether someone is safe to be seen on the basis of information, not principles about labelling people. This is not an area for you to take risks – there are plenty of others where you can. Reluctant clients do include people who have the kind of symptoms which result in behaviour they cannot control, who are desperately angry that you have been forced on them, or who are out of control through alcohol or drugs.

Being safe also applies to keeping yourself away from situations which make you vulnerable to accusation, be it sexual abuse, fraud, unprofessional conduct, or neglect. It follows that all kinds of 'playing at being friends' are no-go areas. Having coffee with someone in a public, and therefore a relatively safe, environment, where the purpose is very definitely to talk over the thing you are meeting about, can be very helpful; an intimate dinner for two 'after work' is definitely not.

The computer has revolutionised our lives, and made it much easier for workers and service users to find essential information. The following may not be necessary advice if you are a seasoned computer user, but just in case: the web has many fraudsters, unscrupulous sexual predators and time wasters, as well as the many useful and worthwhile services it provides. It is part of our role to teach and protect service users.

Before seeing the client you need to make a risk assessment. This is likely to be formalised by your agency; if so you will have some form filling to do. If you find this a tedious waste of time, it is worth remembering that such procedures grew out of tragedies which happened partly because there were no safety nets. Involve the client – this is all part of building a relationship.

Think about what you wear: for example scarves and long earrings can be grabbed.

In every case, not just when meeting risky contacts, colleagues should know where you are at all times, and when they expect to hear from you again.

HOME OFFICE GUIDELINES
General personal safety
Reminder: these are not a substitute for agency policies.

- Get a personal attack alarm from a DIY store or ask your local crime prevention officer where you can buy one. Carry it in your hand so you can use it immediately to scare off an attacker. Make sure it is designed to continue sounding if it is dropped or falls to the ground.

- Carry your house keys in your pocket. If someone grabs your bag, let it go. If you hang on, you could get hurt. Remember your safety is more important than your property.

- If you think someone is following you, check by crossing the street, more than once if necessary to see if the following continues. If you are still worried, get to the nearest place where there are other people, a pub or anywhere with a lot of lights on, and call the police. Avoid using an enclosed phone box in the street, as the attacker could trap you inside.

- If you regularly go jogging or cycling, try to vary your route and time. Stick to well-lit roads with pavements. On commons and parklands, keep to main paths and open spaces where you can see and be seen by other people; avoid wooded areas.

- If you wear a personal stereo, remember you can't hear traffic, or somebody approaching behind you.

- Don't take short-cuts through dark alleys and parks or across waste ground.

- Walk facing the traffic so a car cannot pull up behind you unnoticed.

- If a car stops and you are threatened, scream and shout, and set off your personal attack alarm if you have one. Get away as quickly as you can. This will gain you vital seconds and make it more difficult for the car driver to follow. If you can, make a mental note of the number and description of the car. Write down details as soon as possible afterwards.

- Don't hitch-hike or take lifts from strangers.

- Cover up expensive-looking jewellery.

- Self-defence and safety awareness classes may help you feel more secure. Ask your local police or your work if they have classes.

(Home Office 2008)

Inside the home or establishment

- State clearly who you are, and why you are there.

- Make note of all exits to rooms.

- Stay near the outside door.

- Keep your car keys where they are immediately available if home visiting.

- When there is a concern about violence or you do not know the client well, never conduct an interview in the kitchen.

- Allow people to blow off steam, but don't allow emotion to escalate.

- Do not allow the desire to help override caution.

- Keep well out of arm's reach.

- If someone is angry, don't make sustained eye-to-eye contact.

- Don't corner the person or block their escape route – but do look after your own!

- Don't approach too close.

- Leave if you are scared.

(Home Office 2008)

. . . .

Exercise: Clues and comeback

Here are some client behaviours which could lead to aggression and violence. How would you respond helpfully to each of the following?

Clues for possible escalation of aggression

1. Repeated succession of questions

2. Using another language in an aggressive manner

3. Using obscenities or sarcasm

4. Shouting

5. Replying abruptly or refusing to reply

6. Rapid breathing

7. Pacing

8. Clenched fist or pointing fingers

9. Invading your personal space

10. Staring

11. Tight jaw with clenched teeth

12. Shoulders squared up and dominating

Here are some examples of suggested responses:

Warning signs/cues of violence – responses that may help diffuse aggression

1. Repeated succession of questions
   Appear calm, self-controlled and confident, confirming that you are addressing their concerns.

2. Using another language in an aggressive manner
   Identify language origin and locate interpreter to assist if you possibly can.

3. Using obscenities or sarcasm
   Do not match their language.

4. Shouting
   Ask for information with a calm voice.

5. Replying abruptly or refusing to reply
   Calmly confirm the received information back to the aggressor.

6. Rapid breathing
   Breathe slowly and evenly.

7. Pacing
   Attempt to sit them comfortably.

8. Clenched fist or pointing fingers
   Do not fold your arms or clench your fists in reaction.

9. Invading your personal space
   Maintain a comfortable distance.

10. Staring
    Maintain normal but broken eye contact.

11. Tight jaw with clenched teeth
    Open hands to the aggressor.

12. Shoulders squared up and dominating.
    Stand to the side.

(Substantially obtained from
Gloucestershire Hospitals NHS Trust 2003)

Comment

How many did you know? In spite of what is often said, responses are not common sense – in some of the situations you model the behaviour you want the person to adopt, and in others, you do exactly the opposite. These are things which need to be learned and practised, so that you can use them when feeling scared and under pressure.

. . . .

Finally, in my experience, more assaults have happened in unexpected situations such as being accosted in the corridor of a hostel by a complete stranger, with your own client innocently in his own room. The moral of this has to be: always maintain an appropriate wariness – it will not detract from being warm and friendly.

Summary

- It is important to strike a balance between responsible risk and over-concern.
- Clients are violent for many different reasons.
- We must keep ourselves safe by careful preparation for any contact with a client.
- We must follow both general safety guidelines and those set by our workplace.
- We need to recognise both verbal and non-verbal clues.
- There are ways of diffusing aggression.

FURTHER INFORMATION

Suzy Lamplugh Trust (2009) *Personal Safety at Work: A Guide for Everyone.* London: Suzy Lamplugh Trust.

10. Making Contact with Clients

Making a date with someone is not as simple as it seems...

...your good intentions may not be well received.

HOW TO BEGIN

How do you make contact with someone – by letter, phone, personal meeting or email? It is worth spending a little time on this topic, as the quality of your first approach may win or lose you the battle to speak to someone who does not actually want you.

A well-known authority, Albert Mehrabian (1972), suggests that 7 per cent of our communication comes through the words we say, 38 per cent through the way we say them, and 55 per cent through our facial expression. Though his book is over 30 years old, it is a classic, and you will find it referred to in modern works.

So a letter to someone may be effective because it is not 'loaded' with appearances, but it is obviously very impersonal. Often professional people are surprised and affronted when there is no response to their carefully constructed letter. If Mehrabian is somewhere near right, that our letter has only communicated 7 per cent of what we want to get over, which is to be welcoming and friendly, our reluctant client is far more likely to put the letter in the bin than to respond to it.

The telephone allows us to convey warmth in our voice, to respond helpfully to the client's response to our call, and to forge some kind of bond through conversation. However, we are lacking over half our tools for establishing rapport – our facial expressions – on the telephone. No doubt this will change in centuries to come if the online camera becomes as common as the phone is today!

You may conclude that the personal meeting is by far the most effective for first contacts. However, it is good to remember that an unannounced call is generally discourteous, and only justified in conditions of extreme emergency, danger, or actual need to apprehend someone who may abscond. The vast majority of situations do not fall into these categories, so the phone or letter will usually have had to be risked first. My experience is that it is amazing how many potential clients will give the new visitor a chance even if they are very suspicious of 'help', sometimes with very good reason.

Email has widened our repertoire, and has a number of its own strengths and weaknesses:

- It is quick, easy and requires less effort for the recipient than replying to a letter.

- The growth of the chat room as a method for people to support each other shows that some people feel comfortable with this kind of contact.

However, researchers at Curtin University of Technology (2006) have pointed out a few hazards, which are unique to this form of written communication. They discourage use of **bold**, CAPITALS and colours, which give the sense of shouting at people from the screen. On the positive side, it is worth consulting their site to learn some useful informal devices – if you are young you will probably know all about this! I feel that email has helpfully done away with some of the stuffier conventions of formal letters, but respect must always be the guiding principle.

If you put pressure on people to see you at your convenience, poor results may follow. There is a very real difficulty here: in these days of services under pressure, juggling all sorts of responses, you simply do not have the flexibility you would like. For me this has meant evening visits when I would have preferred to be doing something else, as it is particularly important for clients who have managed to find work to be fully supported by not having to take time off. Many involuntary clients are of course 'captive' during the day – this makes life a little easier for helpers!

SOME OTHER CONSIDERATIONS

These may not be obvious. In my first years of working, I wish I had been aware of many stumbling blocks based around race and culture, over which I fell and hurt both myself and my clients, without understanding why. Recent works have addressed both race and gender, as well as the basics of interview skills, so if I had had access to *Interviewing: A Practical Guide for Students and Professionals* by Keats (2000), for example, I might have known that, in many cultures, it is less than acceptable to:

- send a woman to interview a man

- send a man to interview a woman

- interview a married woman alone, or without her husband being present

- send a person of one religion to interview a person of a different religion when there is conflict between the two religious groups

- mention the names of people who have recently died

- look directly into a person's face when speaking

- cause the listener to lose face.

Obviously these examples do not apply to everyone whose racial background is not Western. Also, you and your client do not necessarily have a choice about working together, nor about the content of the discussion. However, it makes all the difference in the world if you know you are having to act offensively. First of all you may be able to make significant changes such as taking someone with you with whom your client will feel comfortable. If no change is possible you can convey to him or her that you are sorry that a more appropriate person is not available, and that you need to raise very difficult matters.

Sometimes work which has been done to improve services for people with specific conditions can help us more generally, especially where involuntary clients are concerned. For example, the question of home visits:

> Some people really do need to be seen at home, if possible, for example people with dementia. Familiarity is imperative to a person with dementia feeling safe and comfortable. Be sure that the environment is free from noise, interruptions and distractions: i.e. is quiet, pleasant and calm. People with dementia, because of their deficits, have heightened sensitivity to other people's moods, feelings, body language and tones of voice. Before interviewing the person with dementia, take a minute to breathe deeply, close your eyes and picture the two of you having relaxed communication with a positive outcome. Enter the person's space as a friend, with a warm smile and relaxed demeanour. The person needs reassurance and understanding in order to communicate with you. (Wisconsin Department of Health and Family Services 2002, p.5)

This is relevant to many people who are more terrified than you think, especially if they have an inkling that you are going to take them away from their familiar surroundings. In any case your assessment will be much more detailed and useful if made in a home context.

When you are making contact with a child, who is always in a sense an involuntary client, remember that children cannot communicate effectively in a formal language-based interview. The child's primary language is the language of play, with toys, drawing books and stories, which can act as vehicles for communication and bridges to the child's experience (Bayliss 1998, p.35). Bayliss suggests that you move to the child's level, physically, and kneel on the floor rather than sit behind a desk. Introduce yourself and your function in words the child can understand.

Now for a little practical application:

. . . .

Exercise: Mr and Mrs Sunderland

Mr and Mrs Sunderland are in their eighties and have daily help from a home warden. You are the new worker. Their previous worker, Carmen Rainier, was unable to introduce you personally to the Sunderlands before she left, but promised that you would write a letter of introduction. The case notes are brief, but you read of complaints relayed via the warden that Mr Sunderland has struck his wife on two occasions, but no note of this being discussed. Mr Sunderland has complained about damp in the council flat and the previous worker has written a memo to the Housing Department about this.

Here are four sample letters; read each and make a small list of comments about them in the light of your own experience and the points made in this chapter.

Letter 1

Dear Edith,

I'll be in your neighbourhood and I'd like to pop in to say hello and talk about the damp. If there are any other problems, it'll be fine to talk about those, too. I can also bring some info about local day centres and volunteer help groups.

I hope Tuesday the 17th at about 3 in the afternoon suits; look forward to seeing you then.

Don't wait in specially; I'll call back if you're out.

Chris Brown

Letter 2

Ms Edith Sunderland, CONFIDENTIAL c/o the Day Centre

Dear Ms Sunderland,

My colleague mentioned your difficulties with your husband and asked if I could make contact to see if I can help in any way.

I will be calling at the Day Centre on Tuesday afternoon and Aisha Ryan is happy for us to use the quiet room if you'd like to talk things over. Aisha can join us if you'd like that.

I look forward to meeting you on Tuesday.

Yours sincerely,

Jay Khan
Social worker (student)

Letter 3

Dear Mr and Mrs Sunderland,

I am Pat Jones and I am a student social worker at Town Social Services, where Carmen Rainier used to work. Carmen asked if I could get in touch, and I wonder if it would be convenient for me to call on Tuesday (the 17th) at 3.00 pm? I'm looking forward to meeting you both and I hope I can be of help.

Pat Jones,
Student social worker

Letter 4

Dear Mr and Mrs Sunderland,

I work in the same office as Ms Rainier, who left for another post. Unfortunately, she had a few crises in her last week, so could not introduce me to you personally.

I know you are experiencing some difficulties and I would like to call to see if there is anything I can do. Perhaps we can look at your problems, focus on one and work to achieve a goal?

Please telephone to tell me if it's convenient to call on 17 November at 3.00 pm.

Yours faithfully,

P. Smith
Social Worker Supervisor

Compare our lists

I would be interested in your list, especially points which I have not mentioned. My comments are as follows:

Letter 1

Use of first name is disrespectful without permission, especially to an older person.

You haven't introduced yourself.

'Pop in' demeans the visit and is untrue.

It is good to mention the damp, as something the clients have actually requested help about.

Don't hint at 'other problems' with reluctant clients who don't know you.

Trying to be informal by saying that it does not matter if clients are not in demeans the service and is wasteful of your (and the service's) time.

Should you say what your role is?

Letter 2

You haven't introduced yourself.

You tried to offer privacy.

An honest approach, but the client would feel very threatened that a very sensitive matter, which the file said hadn't been discussed with her, is being exposed in writing like that, especially as she does not know you. It is good to involve the worker whom the client knows.

My colleagues have never been able to agree whether or not you should say you are a student in an introductory letter. On the one hand it is honest to do so, on the other it can put clients off, as they assume – wrongly (!) – that they will get a second class service from a student. Sometimes the word trainee has a much better image. What do you think?

Letter 3

It is good to link to the previous worker.

You haven't said the purpose of your visit, but perhaps the client can assume this from the link with the previous worker. There is a touch of warmth in the last sentence.

Letter 4

An attempt at honesty and clarity, but are you sure the clients know the previous worker has left? A bad way to learn if not? They certainly do not need to hear about 'a few crises' – a plain apology would be much better in this context.

'Some difficulties' will threaten the clients – much better to focus on the damp.

'Perhaps we can look at your problems, focus on one and work to achieve a goal?' – is dreadful social work/management speak!

'Yours faithfully' is hardly ever used nowadays, and certainly not in a letter which addresses the clients by name. It is debatable whether to sign oneself 'Social Worker Supervisor', immediately raising the question for the clients, 'Why is the boss coming?' Combined with the jargon, it is an off-putting communication overall.

Now recall the content of this chapter and consider the following:

- Is a letter the best method of contacting these clients, or would some other means be better?

- Did you assume these clients are white? If not, would there be any dilemma about Letter 2? You may be balancing a breach of etiquette in some cultures by interviewing a wife without her husband, against the need to protect her.

This exercise is adapted from one by two respected social work teachers, Doel and Shardlow (2005) – full reference in the 'Further information' section below. I have used it with great success with students and it is free and available for you on the web. Like all simple exercises, it raises far more issues than you might have imagined.

• •

ROUND UP

Concluding this one: you will never be in a position to respond accurately to all members of different races, identity or social classes, nor be completely accepted as one of their own, but you can show sensitivity by recognising that there are very different interpretations of even the simplest gesture or word. The more you can communicate sincerely to people that you understand their reservations about seeing you, the better your success rate is likely to be.

It gets easier:

> Don't introduce me to that man! I want to go on hating him, and I can't hate a man whom I know. (Charles Lamb 1800, in Zuck 1997, p.188)

Summary

- Making contact with someone is a complex matter which needs much thought.
- Explore some of the different meanings which different cultures may place on the same 'ice breaking' action before proceeding.
- Some ways of establishing rapport are more effective than others.
- Introductory letters can be more or less effective, depending on how you have worded them.

FURTHER INFORMATION

Doel, M. and Shardlow, S. (2005) *Modern Social Work Practice*. Farnham: Ashgate.

11. Contracts

What do you do after you have said hello...

...make a contract!

WHY?

As helpers, we can be our own worst enemies. In order to try to be friendly, unintimidating and informal, we sometimes leave our clients nonplussed about our purpose. Howe (1990), on the basis of his research, said that clients felt confused, baffled and irritated by social workers who did not make their agendas clear. For reluctant clients, add a big element of fear of our intentions.

RELUCTANT CLIENTS ARE NOT KEEN ON CONTRACTS!

There is a bit of a dilemma here – having acknowledged that it is important to be clear and honest, the standard way of setting 'goals' (as parodied in the *Mr and Mrs Sunderland* exercise) is hardly likely to be popular with involuntary clients. Research by Dr Judith Cingolani (1993, p.5) has shown that we simply start too early: 'Trying to negotiate contracts in the first interview, a common practice in child welfare protective services, usually doesn't work and often intensifies conflict.' We often think we are operating gently, but our language is less than helpful: 'We have had a report that you are harming your children' is not a good beginning. You may feel that this is an extreme example – no one would start like that – not only have I heard something like it many times, but these words are a direct quotation from the research of Gough (1993, p.8), who made a study of the ways children's service workers routinely introduced themselves to clients. He also says that European child protection workers are much better than British workers at the introduction of sensitive topics like this.

What helps is to ask clients what they imagine we have come for, then state our purpose in as few words as possible. If we are there to supervise, it is much better to be honest than to pretend we have just dropped in. Next it is useful to agree on how the meetings will go, how long they will normally last, and what the client hopes to gain from them. A negative or angry answer to the last is to be expected, but it is important as a chance to ask what *could* help. For example, a young man who could not leave his house was asked if there was anything at all which would make it easier for him to get out. His reply was quite simple: 'try after dark'. Fortunately this conversation happened to take place in the winter! However, I wanted the young man to succeed so much I would have been prepared to take him out at 11 pm in midsummer. There is a solution to most things!

INFORMAL CONTRACTS

The above forms the beginning of a contract of sorts. What definitely does not work is for the helper to decide the aims without consultation with the client. But, I hear you saying, isn't that precisely what work with involuntary clients is all about: forcing things on people who do not want them? My experience is that the 'force' element is actually very small – simply that you are in contact. The rest is actually much more negotiable and open-ended than this. If it isn't, the client will no doubt be living in a setting which is protective to both him or her and you.

One thing which can make the client feel freer is not to ask hundreds of questions, unless of course that is the precise purpose of your visit, which would have been stated at the beginning. Instead, it is better to observe and listen. If clients feel that you are not going to interrogate them, they are far more likely to open up. As an example, I had a job which required me to do a monitoring visit every fortnight. I found that, rather than go through a tedious routine of asking the client each week how he or she felt, what had been happening, and so forth, it worked to agree from the outset that worker and client would bring items to their meetings which each wished to talk about, and that there would be no 'small talk'. It was surprising how much the clients put on the agenda – at other times the meeting would last only ten minutes.

It is essential to address the matter of confidentiality at the outset. Many workers are uncomfortable about this, fearing that their relationship with the client will suffer if they tell him or her that their discussions are not confidential. It is certainly the case that there are some agencies whose strength is that they preserve confidentiality whatever is revealed. I cannot help feeling that there must be some dilemmas for such agencies: for example, is it really feasible not to pass on knowledge of a murder? As far as involuntary clients are concerned, I feel it is more helpful to say that everything is potentially shared with colleagues, because of the need to work as a team.

The ramifications of confidentiality do not end with the client. Workers need to talk to their supervisors: the issues are exactly the same as for client relationships. I remember working with a student who insisted that all supervisory discussions must be confidential – he and I simply had to agree to differ!

FEELINGS

Most helpers acknowledge the importance of clients' feelings. This is not the same as seeing these feelings as valid:

> Practitioners often defined clients' perceptions of the situation as self-serving or irrelevant. If they dealt with them at all, it was usually to attempt to persuade clients that their perceptions were wrong. (Cingolani 1993, p.4)

You can expect conflict:

> There is nothing inherently bad about conflict, and attempts to avoid it during contracting are naive. When contracting goes too smoothly, it is often a sign that one side is selling out to the other or has a hidden agenda. Differences must be teased out and negotiated, and the sooner the differences are revealed the better it is for the process. Less waste of time and energy! (McDonald 2001, pp.2–3)

WHAT ABOUT OTHER PEOPLE?

'Is it the expectation of the helping organisation that the target for change will always be the client?' asks the above expert (p.2). 'What consideration are significant others and environmental systems given in the change process?' He says that it is helpful to make it clear that you will be working with other people for his or her benefit: the family, school, court, financial agencies or other significant people. This can take the pressure off the reluctant client or, conversely, make him or her feel threatened. If so, it is especially important that things which are non-negotiable, for example court orders, are made clear. In such cases we are always required to work as a team with others. However, McDonald does conclude that, if relationships are bad between your client and the 'others', be they agencies or family, your work could be sabotaged. So it is worth putting in a great deal of effort with people who surround the client.

Sharing of information is a particularly difficult issue, but is crucial to the overall care of the client. Not being involved increases feelings of isolation, grief and loss which are common to many carers. I have heard something like the following many times where the client has a mental health problem: 'Her doctor will not discuss her condition with me and I need to understand it so that I know how to help.'

Many carers do not realise that the patient must give consent before any information can be shared – it can be a feature of the illness that their loved one needs to reject them. Your role is vital here, namely:

- to be a 'go between', respecting the confidentiality of both client and family members, and offering support

- to bring people together at a point where the client is not acutely ill

- to ask the client what may be recorded about helping him or her if he or she is too ill to co-operate.

A useful example which 'normalises' this is to explain to client and carer that, when someone has diabetes, the carer has to force them to take sugar or insulin, otherwise they may lapse into a coma and die – an act of love, not dictatorship…

The above examples come from mental health practice, but the principles are the same for all work.

HIDDEN AGENDAS

A common way of operating is what Seabury (1976, p.16) refers to as the 'corrupt contract'. This is when the worker or client proceeds without explicitly stating an objective – a hidden agenda. Although the idea is old, I have found that hidden agendas are very much alive and well!

I am ready to stick my neck out and say that, in certain circumstances, hidden agendas are not always wrong: an example being when you might take a child on an outing where you have arranged for some prospective foster carers 'accidentally' to be present. However, the meeting is not a contract, only the outing.

The problem with a corrupt contract is that sooner or later the hidden agendas are discovered and the work is ruined when people realise they have been deceived.

What may be interesting is looking at some *hidden* hidden agendas – the ones we did not know were there.

. . . .

Exercise: House rules

You could do this on your own, but it would be better in a group – family or workplace. If either of the latter, note that this can be an intense exercise, so leave plenty of time for discussion and support.

Explain that all families and teams develop a set of 'rules' which can be very powerful, even though people are often unaware of them and they are certainly not written down! As far as teams are concerned, these are in addition to the formal policies and rules. Examples:

- Never sit in the boss's chair in the office.

- Don't eat at your desk.

- Always offer to make a cup of coffee for others when making one for yourself.

Proceed as follows:

1. As a group, think about life in your team during an ordinary day. Make a list of 'rules' which you think operate in the team.

2. Read out what everyone has written.

3. Think about how each rule came into being, and what, if anything, should be done about each one. Is it reasonable to have some unwritten rules in a team which are accepted and not questioned?

4. Discuss how many of the rules are positive.

Discussion

'House rules' are an inevitable part of group life. Frequently they are useful: for example most people feel uncomfortable if they think they are wrongly dressed for an event. Some people take pleasure in breaking the rules. What definitely causes distress is breaking rules which you did not know existed, a bit like swimming in a clear blue sea which has treacherous undercurrents. On the other hand, rules like bringing cake on someone's birthday are fun and enhance team life.

It may be helpful in understanding all this to refer to Transactional Analysis (Cryer 1990). This theory suggests that all young individuals learn certain ways of feeling and behaving which become habitual when they are older – 'a life-script'. One individual's script is very different from another's because of differences in how they were treated in early life by people they relied on and learned from (Cryer 1990, p.368). Individuals are seldom aware of their scripts because these are so much part of them that they do not normally consider examining them, and they might even have difficulty in teasing out what they are. So house rules are generally unwritten. They often aim at making individuals more comfortable: sometimes this is at the expense of others. How far do the rules you have teased out enable people, or do some of them make some members seem more powerful than they really are?

• •

SUMMING UP

Returning to your agreements with clients: have you or they unwittingly applied a few rules which are getting in the way? This includes things like: 'The previous worker always did it this way,' 'I need a cigarette after one hour.'

Finally, if you hate contracts, it is worth remembering times when you felt in a situation where you did not know what was expected of you – what would have helped? I have found that offering reluctant clients the simple aim *'Get rid of me'* is not as flippant as it sounds, given that the goal of many social care contracts is to make oneself redundant.

Summary

- It is important to be very clear and honest about your purpose in making contact with any client.
- Reluctant clients often do not like formal agreements, so some ways of making informal contracts may be necessary.
- It is essential to take full account of the client's feelings about situations.
- The client's and your professional networks need to be included in the contract.
- Our real agendas with people may be hidden: this has important implications.
- There are often powerful hidden agendas in the workplace team.

FURTHER INFORMATION

Trotter, C. (2006) *Working with Involuntary Clients.* Crows Nest, Western Australia: Allen and Unwin.
   Pages 117–118 are particularly relevant.

12. Recording

Anything you say may be taken in evidence...

...this is nearly always true.

EVIDENCE – AGAINST OR FOR

It is hardly surprising that involuntary clients feel threatened by workers' and organisations' written records, and that they often assume that they are going to be condemned by what is set in print – my experience is that many written records are quite unbelievably bad in their condemnatory, biased and inaccurate way of describing people and events. This is a shame because written work can be a brilliant tool for helping the reluctant client to feel more confident.

All of us are obviously sensitive about what is in our records, and involuntary clients particularly so. I can only remember one client who did not wish to see what was written about her. She felt so desperate about her badness she could not believe that there could be anything good in her file.

Accuracy in recording is not as easy as it sounds. A useful little exercise is to estimate the percentage of inaccuracy you think there is in eyewitness accounts of events, especially where the situation is emotionally charged (*see end of chapter for result*). I am willing to bet that the percentage is more than you thought.

One of the problems of written (now read computer stored) records is the fact that they were traditionally kept from the client. Following the legislation beginning in 1987, which allowed people much more access to their personal files, record keeping improved slightly, but not as much as was needed. Sadly, many organisations complied with the letter of the law, but not its spirit, by making access to files a complicated process, and in some cases a service for which you have to pay. For detailed recent guidance about promoting access to files, you need to read *Your Rights to Personal Files* by the Campaign for Freedom of Information (undated).

Keeping records is one of the differences between 'skilled helping', as defined, and other kinds of friendship. Here there is a very simple guiding principle, which has served me well: never write anything which you would not like to read about yourself. This is as much about the way things are written as the content. It helps your relationship with the client enormously for you to change a word which he or she does not like and for the client to point out a mistake or an omission which has been made – most files provide plenty of scope for this!

However, the client cannot have sole charge of the content of the record. You must note everything which seems important to you, however unpleasant. So there could be occasions where you share with the client a general expression of concern, and discuss the record more fully later. For example, if you intend calling in another professional immediately after you have left the client's home, you may need to be less than open if you believe he or she would disappear if you told him or her what you had decided. Of course your relationship will need some repair after this – most clients will then acknowledge that care sometimes demands extreme measures.

THE LIFE OF A FILE

Now for some practical application – imagine yourself in the following scenarios.

You work in a residential drug rehabilitation unit. You are key worker to Ann, an Asian woman aged 31, who has a mild learning disability. She is in a relationship with Len, a white man aged 35, who is also a resident, and the couple appear to be mutually supportive. This afternoon Ann told you that Len had brought cannabis into the unit and offered some to her. She asks you what to do, and begs you not to tell anyone, as Len has threatened to tell her family that she is receiving treatment if she does. You want to encourage Ann to maintain her partnership with Len, but now have some doubts in view of the information she has given. You now have to act in accordance with procedure.

You would need to tell Ann you will share the information and the reasons for this. Then you would tell your manager what Ann has said, so that together you can be clear on agency policy. It could be that bringing in drugs means expulsion for Len, or that he is given a warning. You write up the incident in Ann's file first and Len's second.

You have known Ann for six months and she has shared many of her problems with you, including the fact that she was sexually abused by her father when she was eight. Recently she asked to look at her file.

You look at Ann's file to see if it is suitable for her to read. You would be checking how to handle the reading, not whether or not Ann could see the file, even if the contents were unpleasant. The Data Protection Act 1998 says that requests may be made by the individuals to whom the contents relate irrespective of age or any other criteria. In cases where people are incapable of understanding or exercising their rights, for instance because they are too young or suffer from a severe mental disability, then subject access requests may be made by parents or other persons who are legally able to act on their behalf. If Ann is able to read, what is her preferred language? Did you make any assumptions about her based on her cultural background?

Before arranging a file reading with Ann, you would need to be aware that access to file requests must be made to representatives of the holders of the information, who are allowed up to 40 days in which to respond. There are cases where it is legitimate to share information without a person's knowledge or consent. This could well apply to Len's bringing of drugs to the centre (Information Commissioner's Office 2008).

Ensuring confidentiality where necessary is complicated. For example, if Len were to ask for access to his file, the fact that Ann had disclosed to staff the information that he had brought drugs to the centre would be withheld – this is clearly information for the confidential section of the file. However, his records could be examined by the police if a case is brought against him.

Your organisation should make sure that you understand all provisions for the safe storing of information, with special attention to your friend the computer. The consequences of Ann or Len's file being lost are potentially very serious; during times of such limbo, many service users try to kill themselves. At best, you could be the subject of disciplinary action.

This cautionary tale may have raised your anxiety level. The thing to remember is that it is the employer's responsibility to ensure that team members know how to handle both recording systems and files. If you are employed you need to consult agency policies very thoroughly; if not refer to the 'Further information' section at the end of the chapter.

Recording is a skill that helpers often 'learn by doing' without any training. Perhaps this is why many files are not clear, are full of jargon, and include the kinds of statement one would not like written about oneself. Of course records need to be accurate – indeed it is vital that they should be – but there is a way of writing which is sensitive. The guiding principle is, 'How would I like this to be written about me?' With this in mind, try the following:

. . . .

Exercise: Other people's records!

Translate these statements which have been found in actual records (not yours!) into the kind of statements you would like to see about yourself:

1. Trisha is aggressive and self-centred.

2. Mrs Khan presents in a hostile manner.

3. There is an ongoing conflict situation.

4. He is inadequate.

5. The family has a lot of inner resources.

6. They have rejected him.

7. He is a difficult case.

8. Mr Davy is a needy, dependent enuretic.

9. Samantha is an acting-out attention seeker.

10. Sean must prove he responds to structure.

11. Winston is over-sensitive about his colour.

12. George represses his emotions.

13. Mr Pradish is uncommunicative.

14. Polly is very demanding.

15. Claire laughs and dresses inappropriately.

(Substantially obtained from Doel and Shardlow 1993)

Comment

I am willing to bet, unless you have had some training, you can't see anything wrong with some of these statements, or are unable to rewrite them. Some of them are even attempting to be positive about people! My experience is that many workers have learned this style from files, so, not surprisingly, think this is the way to write. If you are very new to this kind of work you may be in a better position to see that these are judgemental, jargonistic, 'labelling' sorts of record.

Supposing we were to add to the first principle, 'Write it as you would like it written about you,' another which says, 'Always describe behaviour, not make general statements,' and another which says, 'Make it clear when you are giving your own opinion.'

Here are some observations on some of the statements:

Statement 1

For Statement 1, you might say: 'I noticed that Tricia shouted at another resident when he changed over the television programme without asking her.' This takes more words but gives the reader a picture of what happened. If a similar incident happens every hour and is recorded accurately, it is very much easier for staff to discuss Tricia's behaviour with her, showing her the records of some 20 incidents when she has become angry, and for any external colleague to assess the situation. If situations are accurately described, a better picture of the whole situation emerges. It could be that Tricia has every right to be angry if she is being picked on by someone, or that she is generally unhappy and upset about her life.

Statement 5

'The family has a lot of inner resources' sounds like a compliment, but what does it actually mean? Much better to make a list of the family's strengths, which might go something like this:

- Everyone in the family does something to help Peter, who needs someone to hand him his clothes, take him to the loo and cut up his food each day.

- Peter's parents spend time with each of their children each day, to ensure they do not feel left out.

- The parents attend all meetings where Peter is concerned, which must be difficult in view of the other demands on their time.

The writer may have meant something entirely different by the statement, such as the faith which sustains family members, or the calm way all family members behave even under stress.

Statement 11

'Winston is over-sensitive about his colour.' Again, there is no evidence for this statement. Does it mean that he becomes angry if he feels that people are being racist? If so, this is not over-sensitivity. It may be that he needs the support of a black worker, if the environment he is in is predominantly white. White workers often, in my experience, criticise black people for being 'over-sensitive'. This is because many black people these days challenge jokes and unthinking comments, rather than just accepting them. If the report writer were black there still needs to be a description of Winston's behaviour in its context to make the record credible.

If you feel you agree with these comments, you will see that all the other statements have the same pitfalls. If not, it may be interesting to discuss them with friends or colleagues.

. . . .

RETURNING TO EVIDENCE 'FOR YOU'

Even though there are many considerations, records are wonderful tools for working with reluctant clients. You could start by reading together the client's last formal review, or both of you writing what you think has happened during your current meeting, and sharing the results, even making an application to read the back files. Whatever conflict may arise, should the client disagree with whatever you or others have written, there are excellent opportunities for helping him or her to underline everything positive there is in the file. Obviously you will consider safety, the client's state of mental health and the nature of what is written being of prime importance. I would like to say that dangerousness in itself is not a reason for withholding information; I have experience of sharing records with some of the most dangerous people in England. Obviously safeguards have to be in place for yourself, other people and the client after the session, where there is any question of harm ensuing.

I believe that everything is ultimately useful in working with your reluctant client. The difficult circumstances just described would be excellent material for future meetings; you can read out your clear and accurate account of exactly how you found him or her to be when in a bad state.

Finally, I would like to assure you that the only problems I have ever had with sharing records with clients is the judgemental language found in them – my own and other people's!

Summary

- Records are often seen as a necessary evil, but they can be a positive tool. They need to be both accurate and sensitive.
- There is detailed legal and workplace guidance about the making, storing and sharing of records, which both you and clients need to be aware of.
- Exercise: commonly found unhelpful language in written records.
- Reinforce the place of using records positively with reluctant clients.

FURTHER INFORMATION

O'Rourke, L. and Grant, H. (2005) *It's All in the Record.* Lyme Regis: Russell House Publishing.

Answer for exercise on p.101: Malpass (1996) estimated 85 per cent accuracy in eyewitness accounts.

13. Methods of Helping Suited to the Reluctant Client

You may find that your client is far more interested in the cup of tea served at the group meeting than the subject...

... in fact the cup of tea could be more important.

BEING NORMAL

The challenge of working with people who don't want you is finding ways of operating on an ordinary human level. This sounds pitifully obvious, but in fact many theory books are concerned with methods which are primarily designed for clients who have chosen to accept help, as previously discussed. I have found that a different range of theory is important for the unwilling client. So this is not a chapter about 'methods', it is about using the everyday, even the mundane, to develop our practice.

Maslow (1970), a seminal humanistic writer of the 1970s, set out a 'hierarchy of human needs' which govern our existence, as is shown in the figure below.

*fulfilment
of all
your potential*

respecting yourself and being respected

belonging, love, sex

security, protection, safety

food, drink, warmth, sleep

If as helpers we give the 'obvious' two bottom layers a second look, we may find a useful clue for working with involuntary clients. The particularly pertinent thing which Maslow seemed to emphasise was that the higher needs *cannot* be met until the basic ones have been satisfied. It is true that there have always been men and women who have triumphed over atrocious physical conditions and performed quite staggering feats of heroism or self-education; in my view it is wrong to compare these with anyone else's struggle, which may be, for him or her, just to get through the day. Most people cannot rise to the heights unless they are fed and warm and feel safe.

USING THE EVERYDAY

There is some agreement among practitioners that reluctant clients need something other than structured interviewing to maximise the chances of developing real rapport, for example they are likely to talk about their past when they want to, rather than as part of a structured session. I have found that trying to help such clients to develop insight and make links with the present is rarely helpful – they will gain far more from the humane way you treat them. It follows that trying to help your client understand by explanation why his or her way of life does not work is likely to fail (Keats 2000).

So 'setting goals', a favoured method of social workers, only is effective if the client is truly committed to them, in other words there must be 'something in it' for him or her. This applies as much to case conferences, which are meant to be supportive, but often give the impression that the individual client is seen as the problem, rather than the family or society.

I have also found that formal 'therapeutic' games or exercises rarely work with individuals – excluding ordinary board and card games, which clients can see as 'normal'.

I remember watching a particularly gifted student working: the latter did not ask her client a single question, she simply commented on what she noticed, for example the temperature of the room, the fact that her client looked tired, the ingredients for a meal on the table. In a relaxed interview she had achieved a remarkably full assessment of her quite seriously mentally ill woman's current mood, physical state, and needs.

SOME QUESTIONABLE AIDS

Your client does not want you, so you are doing your best to find a genuine point of contact. What could be more natural than to talk about your own problems as a parent with someone who is being closely supervised, or may have had his or her children placed with foster parents? Or you may be aching to tell someone who is finding it difficult to manage household tasks about your father, who felt just the same about losing independence, and who now loves the services he receives.

On the other hand, you may have taken to heart some of the earlier remarks in this book about informality and personal safety, or have been told that it is always wrong to speak about any of your own experiences, or those of family and friends, to clients because their situation is always different, and even if it isn't, they will never be comforted by the connection.

The case for sharing your own feelings a little, and giving such information as to whether or not you have children, if asked, is generally thought to be friendly and helpful by involuntary clients. But a group of experts, Hepworth, Rooney and Larson (1997), having consulted much research into what best helps reluctant clients in social care, concluded that results were equally divided for and against giving information about yourself. There is not a single view!

So perhaps it is helpful to keep in mind a few questions:

- Who is going to benefit from me talking about myself?

- Am I actually wasting precious time by talking about me?

- Am I avoiding tackling difficult issues?

- Do I want to be liked?

- Am I simply tired and hungry and want to go home?

The use of humour is mentioned by several experts as being useful with involuntary clients. For example, Lawrence Schulman (1991) found that child protection workers who had a sense of humour were more likely to be viewed by their clients as helpful, skilful and trustworthy. Later another two experts, Pollio (1995) and Struthers (1999), who both worked in the statutory sector, tell of situations where humour which is directly related to the situation in hand can be very helpful in taking the heat out of things. Both writers caution against telling jokes, and discourage anything which could be demeaning to the client. I am sure you will have direct experience of all these kinds of humour from your schooldays, when you were yourself an involuntary client! Certainly I have always found myself on safest ground when I use humour against myself. For example, a young client once told me he would like to see X. I replied that sounded a good idea, what about inviting him to tea? It quickly transpired that X was a well-known pop star. This gaffe, which the young person never allowed me to forget, forged a new bond between us.

USING CRISES

What many people think of as a problem is in fact a dangerous opportunity

When I was training, I noticed for the first time how clients in hospital seemed particularly receptive to my efforts to help. This could be explained somewhat negatively by the fact that being ill makes people so low and lacking in resistance that they will do anything you ask, or that the authority structure in a hospital is so intimidating that clients dare not resist.

Another, somewhat more optimistic way of thinking is the idea that being in hospital is always a crisis. Our society usually uses the word 'crisis' as a negative term, but most people would also recognise events like leaving home, getting married, having a baby or even going on holiday as having some of the elements of crisis. According to the *Chambers Dictionary* (Chambers 2003, p.357) the word 'crisis' means a crucial or decisive moment. We seem to be more receptive to change at times of crisis because we struggle to maintain our balance at such times, our adrenalin perhaps flows more freely, and we are capable of all sorts of efforts we could not normally make; for example, the person who is afraid of flying who takes the aeroplane to Australia to visit his sick brother.

It is this receptivity which is very helpful to you and your reluctant client. By the nature of the work, having services imposed nearly always happens at a crisis point; obviously the event itself could be any one of a number of horrible things: being diagnosed with a life-threatening illness, going to prison, the death of someone dear, even having you imposed upon them! In order to cope, your client tries to fall back on whatever he or she has done before when threatened. These 'strategies' vary from the very helpful, such as finding out lots of information about the situation he or she is in, to the more unhelpful like drink or illegal drugs. If there is someone like you around after the crisis, the client is more likely to use this chance of a sounding board, rather than rush into unconstructive action because of the degree of distress or fear surrounding him or her.

Supposing you have learned a few tried and tested ways of responding to your client, you have a much better chance of using the crisis to its full potential for him or her to cope better with life generally. I, along with a colleague, Nigel Horner, an inspired social work teacher, devised the following list of useful tips from our reading and experience:

1. Give the client as much information as you can. This could include finding out about particular conditions or illnesses, arranging for him or her to see other professionals, or making visits to care homes. It is really important not to withhold difficult information, unless the client, the needs of others or his or her condition really does preclude this. You will always be imparting problem information in conjunction with, or in the presence of, other professionals.

2. Use pictures, leaflets, the web and other aids to communication. Information makes more sense if it can be referred to again and again, as the person may be too shocked to take it in at first.

3. Try to enlist the support of others, such as family, a team or a network. Many family reconciliations take place as a result of crisis, and perhaps for the first time your client may actually gain comfort from association with people who have similar problems.

4. Ask the person what has helped before when he or she has been in crisis. This is an important point, as we often assume others have the same strategies as ourselves. For example, I remember a clergyman who simply could not understand why a newly bereaved person he was visiting would prefer to watch her favourite soap rather than talk to him.

5. Allow plenty of time for people in shock. As you may know from your own experience, people in shock often cannot accomplish the simplest task or take in a single word.

6. Stay with the pain. Physically, this means choosing the setting which will be most comforting for the service user, not yourself. An example which springs to mind was when a young service user insisted on asking very sensitive questions of the author in the crowded waiting room of a court. The noise and

hubbub, combined with the crisis of court attendance, helped the young man to feel less naked in his discomfort.

7. Acknowledge that this is a terrible situation, which may be unresolvable. This is suitable in very negative situations, where the same type of crisis has occurred over and over again. You will need to feel confident in using this approach, but the following example may ring some bells for you: Sophie has run away from her children's home for the eighth time. You suggest to Sophie and the staff team that there is no point in discussing ways to help Sophie to stay as she obviously hates the home and everyone in it. You then ensure that Sophie has the chance to speak first.

8. Make an agreement about who is going to do what. A crisis is a situation where the service user might actually be glad for someone to help out, without taking over completely. For example, a helper could contact family or other professionals, arrange transport or make a cup of tea.

(Substantially obtained from Horner
and Kindred 1997, pp.26–27)

At the risk of stating the obvious – matters are often described as crises when they are actually problems, not things which disturb the client's balance in the way described above. It may well be essential that your client agrees to allow you to have access to his or her finances, but you may have to wait for this information till there is some urgency for that person. I remember one client who needed to be at the point of being evicted from her flat before she could cope with supplying the details which delayed eviction. Needless to say, your organisation will present you with many things which are not crises at all, in the above terms. Example: 'We need these figures now!'

Finally, crisis was described above as a *dangerous* opportunity. The potential is always there for the involuntary client to miss this particular chance by refusing to take medication, running away or being unable to let anyone near his or her pain. Of course some people go to pieces and never recover from a crisis. My father lost his wife early in their marriage, and his life thereafter was a kind of grey monochrome. Just supposing a skilled helper had been at hand to help, I believe the outcome could have been very different.

AN EVERYDAY METHOD

Practitioners speak about 'doing group work' whilst a lot of group work goes on without being thought about, planned or used to its best advantage. I believe that the processes which happen naturally in a group are very useful if they are harnessed and enhanced.

When we experience a group, it is as if all the good and bad things about our society as a whole are also present. For example, group members tend to help each other, but they can also 'gang up' against an unpopular member. Groups can make us feel under pressure, either for good or ill. It is important, therefore, to try to be aware of some of the less obvious pressures which people may be feeling. For instance, women can lack confidence in speaking out, whilst men unconsciously take the lead. If you are the group leader, try to avoid making eye contact mainly with men when starting, giving instructions, ending, and during the group life generally. If there are only a small number of black people present, which is often the case, it is essential that they are not turned to as 'expert' on race. The leader has a responsibility to draw the attention of members to unconscious racism and other forms of prejudice, and not use language which assumes that everyone is heterosexual. Of course other group members should look out for these things too, but the leader tends to be used as a sort of model for everyone else.

Here is a simple way of bringing people together in a group, which is not about sophisticated techniques, rather about bringing out the real feelings which people have – continuing our theme of using the 'ordinary'. You can do this one with colleagues as well as clients – there may be a few surprises!

· ·

Exercise: Agendas

Preparation for group leader to do:

>A piece of paper and biro or pencil for everyone.
>
>Flip chart and pen if possible.
>
>Read instructions below.
>
>Ensure group has half an hour to do the exercise.

Exercise

Explain to group members that you acknowledge that their reasons for being present are many and varied, and that you realise that they may not be present by choice. Since clients have told us over and over again that people do not listen, you are interested in what people really think. Tell them they only have to share with others what they want to. Ask the group members to make two small lists on their paper.

List 1

Write down every reason for being here in this group. Be honest! For example, 'I am here because my social worker said I had to.'

List 2

Note down all the things, large and small, which are on their minds, as well as the groupwork. Nothing is too trivial!

Now explain that you are going to write up on the flip chart paper, or ask people to read out, as many of the things which they have noted and are prepared to share.

Discuss your lists and from it make an agenda for group discussions later. Include everything!

Points for discussion or reflection

The kind of issues which tend to surface are:

'Why I am here'

>I had to come.
>
>I was interested in what the group was about.
>
>I want to get social workers off my back.
>
>I'm a bit bored at the moment, so I need to do something.
>
>I know the person who is leading the group.

I'm not sure really.

I like discussing things in groups.

I want to get my kids back.

'Things, large or small, which are on my mind'

I'm so worried about our son, he seems to be going off the rails.

Did I turn the cooker off?

I must remember to get some vegetables for tomorrow's dinner.

I shall be glad when the divorce is through.

I daren't face going to the doctor with this lump.

Those curtains don't go with the rest of the room.

Now who does she remind me of...?

I wish they would give me a cup of tea.

Is this group part of an assessment?

It's cold in here.

Was this what you found? Were there any other themes?

This exercise builds on people's real agendas, rather than a 'parenting programme' or an 'anger management course'. Those could come later. The group will tackle all the difficult issues in its own good time, when members feel safer, by working round the rather random-looking agenda you have made. People gain much support from being listened to, and by using their own ways of putting things.

. . . .

TO RETURN TO THE 'CUP OF TEA'

Chris Trotter (2006), whose work I have found inspirational in helping me to develop useful methods with people who don't really want intervention, and to understand some of their mind-sets, points out (p.92) that we should be careful of trying to make uncooperative clients change by, for example, conducting the interviews in McDonald's – in other words rewards should come as a result of cooperative behaviour, not in spite of it. Whilst I think we should always steer clear of anything which could be considered a bribe, I would never withhold the refreshments, as I think these lend humanity to work. Even if we have a completely free choice, attending a meeting on a cold day is considerably more attractive if there is a hot drink!

Ways of successful working, then, usually centre round simple things such as shopping, homemaking, clothes, helping your client to feel as safe as possible in his or her environment, and 'life'. There are always exceptions, and I would not wish to appear to denigrate methods which I have enjoyably and productively used with many clients.

Once you know what works, do more of it. (Cade 2007, p.1)

Summary

- Reluctant clients respond best to ordinary, 'human' ways of working with them.
- You can use everyday incidents rather than formal techniques with people.
- Some commonly used devices, such as humour, are questionable, but have their place.
- A crisis in a client's life can be an opportunity to establish rapport with him or her.
- Being part of a group is normal for many clients – this can be used very positively.
- It is possible to engage reluctant clients in groups by focusing on their thoughts during a group meeting.

FURTHER INFORMATION

Centre for Fun and Families (undated) *I've Tried That and It Doesn't Work*. Leicester: Centre for Fun and Families.

This resource booklet offers suggestions and advice to professionals to help overcome feelings of helplessness when working with groups.

14. Good Endings

There are many ways of ending...

...think about these, though.

ENDINGS ARE BEREAVEMENTS

Ending your contact with a client is an experience of loss for you both. This remains true even if the interaction has not been experienced as particularly positive. A leading authority, Murray Parkes (1983), says that, in all situations of loss, grief, anger, guilt and relief may be present, the proportions depending on the quality of the relationship. These feelings often influence the client's signals about ending. Some examples follow.

The client may well drop out, if he or she has a choice. This is distressing, but may not be as negative as it seems, as he or she may be simply avoiding the sadness of ending what was basically a helpful contact. He or she may feel that functioning has improved, and it may not occur to him or her that you have feelings too!

If the client has no choice about whether to see you or not, anger may be the predominating emotion, and this could be expressed in all sorts of ways. Were there non-verbal signals which you have not picked up, such as turning away from you, not speaking, missing appointments? Recognising and acknowledging such feelings can be a help, even if you do not verbalise them with the client. Apparent anger may mask sadness at leaving. Some clients need to 'rubbish' your support; in these circumstances it is not wrong to say what has been valuable for you – so long as you are honest.

For reluctant clients the predominant emotion may well be relief that the unwanted relationship is ending. Rather than feel rejected, celebrate with him or her the positive things which have brought about the end – always remembering to be sensitive about such matters as the severing of a relationship which the client may have valued – even if society and you did not!

GOOD ENDINGS

'The inability to handle termination may sabotage all that has gone before' (Nursten 1997, p.75). Experts stress the importance of ending work because it is so easy to find ways of avoiding the discomfort already described, especially as it is recognised that one of the frustrations of reluctant client work is the fact that we may have to deal with 'one offs', unplanned endings and other unsatisfactory ways of managing work. So try to use whatever degree of control you can, to avoid one more bad severance in what has probably been a long history of these.

If you only have one session with someone, summarising is the key skill of packaging it in easy-to-remember chunks.

In contrast to what has been said earlier, one of the advantages of working with involuntary clients who are confined to care, hospital or prison is that there are regular reviews – use this system to ensure good endings. The purpose of any review is to assess the effectiveness of the care plan and to determine whether any changes to it are required.

At the point of either your personal ending or the goodbye to the physical setting it is vital to introduce the new people or physical environment.

Then there are the little ceremonies you can have. For example, Williams (2001) describes a social work student working with a young person who had experienced many changes in carers and social workers. The student helped the child to realise where they were up to by drawing a picture of two people in a boat; they set off from one island and were rowing to another – each week the boat drew nearer to the other island and waiting at the island was a new social worker.

Sharing your feelings of sadness can be appropriate, so long as you both recognise the professional context of your relationship.

REVIEWS

As with all work of this kind, some kind of evaluation is useful. However, we are unlikely to elicit thanks or much acknowledgement that the period together has been helpful. Over time you may find a consistency about what clients say which is extremely valuable, if not always comfortable! For example many clients have told me that they valued me being honest with them. This inspires one of the key themes of this book.

There are a range of ways of gathering feedback from service users and carers. If you are employed there will be pro formas available, but in all cases, service users and carers should be asked if they are willing to give their views and time taken to explain the reason for their involvement. Methods should be used which are appropriate to individuals' needs. Questions should be in plain English or relevant languages and may be put verbally or in writing, depending on individual circumstances. For children, people with learning difficulties and those who do not use words, games designed for evaluation can be used, for example using smiley faces or number cards as 'rating' measures.

Always remember that service users' feedback may be coloured by the fact that they do not wish to offend, in case they prejudice professionals against them.

THE DOORKNOB SYNDROME

It is well known by counsellors and therapists that a client will often wait until the end of either the session or the contact as a whole before revealing something really important – 'the doorknob syndrome'. There could be two reasons for this: the client hopes to prolong the session or contact, or is scared about telling you something and hopes to escape without discussing it. This is obviously particularly important where involuntary clients are concerned, especially as there is often no choice about being able to see them again. So the 'backstop' arrangements are vital. One of the following could apply:

- You are meeting again and it is a matter which can wait, in which case you say firmly that you will 'put it safely in the fridge till next week'.

- It is something which must be dealt with now, for example an allegation of abuse, where you will have to act, and/or bring someone else in.

- It is important enough to prolong the session, for example 'I have just been told I have cancer,' though in general I believe timetables should be kept to, for the sake of both yourself and your next client.

In all cases you can take some comfort from the fact that the client has gained enough trust to tell you something important.

RECEIVING GIFTS

Present-giving is another important topic which is very controversial, possibly more so where reluctant clients are concerned. A starting point may be that many of us are much happier with giving than receiving in life generally. If so, it is worth wondering why this is.

In order to unpick this issue a little more, imagine that an involuntary client has a small gift-wrapped parcel in his or her hand which he or she is offering to you. Imagine you can stop the clock for a while and ask yourself the following questions:

- What are my feelings about his or her gesture? It is really important to answer this one first, as your feelings may sway your judgement in the wrong direction. The range of feelings goes from pleased and touched through to wary and angry.

- Why does the client want to give me something? If you are worried that there may be an element of a bribe you will obviously refuse as gently and firmly as possible. If you have been working together well, there could be a genuine desire to thank you. It simply does not occur to some people that presents can be seen as bribes.

- Does the organisation I work with have rules about receiving presents? If you are not allowed to accept presents your decision is made for you. Having said that, I feel that a small gift should be accepted, with the explanation that you will need to pass on the present to your boss so that it is shared by others. If you do accept anything, it must always be recorded in your official notes.

There are a lot of 'it depends' yet to be covered:

- Obviously expensive presents and legacies are absolutely out.

- Is the present a coded (or not so coded!) message? One new student found it difficult to see that a gift of six pairs of tights from a man to her, a young woman, may not have been a wise acquisition.

- It is lovely to accept a drink (non-alcoholic) which someone has made for you.

- A client who was obviously wealthy took it in turns with me to buy the drinks when our meetings took place in a coffee bar – this was important in bringing an aspect of equality to the working relationship.

Whatever your conclusions generally, experience does seem to suggest that you consult each client's records well before presents become an issue, as there are safety issues to be considered in addition to all the above. There is a very small minority of people who would deliberately try to poison you, but it is not worth being the target for hatred which is most certainly meant for someone else. This applies to drinks and food which could be laced with something. I remember a colleague being given a cake of the 'hash' variety. We all vary in our tolerance of cups which are not washed as well as we should like – remember you are a helper not a martyr. Having said this, I cannot remember a single instance of being ill from any of the 500 or so drinks I have consumed in clients' homes.

. . . .

Exercise: Gifts

Working on your own or with others, decide which of the following you would accept:

- A cup of tea from someone who is schizophrenic.

- An inexpensive bunch of flowers from a couple whom you are helping to adopt a baby.

- A lift in a client's car.

- A small box of chocolates from someone on probation.

- A bag of sweets from an eight-year-old boy which he tells you he has bought with his own pocket money.

- Flowers from relatives of a terminally ill person whom you have helped to place in a hospice.

No doubt you will feel that all these come into the 'it depends' category, but I cannot resist making a few comments on them!

- People who have schizophrenia may be hospitable or inhospitable, just like anyone else. The only occasions for not accepting would be if the client in question seemed to be very disturbed and was making any comments which suggested they were out of touch with reality. These would definitely be of the 'if in doubt, don't' variety.

- Adoption legal rules state that 'no gifts of cash or kind' may be offered by adoption applicants. I remember being very embarrassed at handing back the couple's gift, as they were both sincere, completely unaware of the implications, just tearful and grateful. Having taken advice, I suggested that a cup of coffee at their expense would be lovely after the final court hearing.

- Accepting lifts would be highly questionable from both a safety and ethics point of view.

- Taking a box of chocolates is definitely in the 'it depends' category. If you are the person writing a report for court on which the client's future depends, this is very different from being the person's care assistant.

- Children are heart-warming in their generosity and it would seem churlish to refuse the present. However, you do need to think about the context. If the child's parent is your involuntary client, proceed with extreme caution, since your acceptance could later be used against you. On the other hand a gift from a child who does not live in his or her own home, and to whom you are a significant adult, is another matter altogether.

- The flowers from grateful relatives are also a third party gift, but acceptance is much less problematic, in my opinion. It can ease pain a little to give something to a helper, however much the latter feels he or she was 'only doing his or her job'.

All these are questionable if the client is involuntary. To sum up: if in doubt – don't!

ENDINGS ARE BEGINNINGS

It would be futile to pretend that all your endings will be positive. However, they are always beginnings – a new worker, a new life, improved practice ensuing from tragedy, a chance that another placement setting may work if this one hasn't... For more, read on!

Summary

- Ending work with a client brings back previous experiences of bereavement for both him or her and the worker.

- There are ways of using endings well or otherwise an inadequate ending practice can sabotage your work. Sometimes we do not have control over this, where involuntary clients are concerned.

- Particular notice needs to be taken of things said by clients at the end of a session or piece of work.

- Present giving and receiving is a vital issue which requires a great deal of thought.

FURTHER INFORMATION

Rogers, V. (2003) *Evaluations and Endings: Activities for Reviewing Work with Young People.* Leicester: National Youth Agency.

15. Rewards

What you sow tends to be what you reap...

...though you won't see the harvest.

WHERE THEN ARE THE REWARDS?

You will find little written about rewards in the helping professions generally: advertisements and recruitment campaigns concentrate on money and 'job satisfaction', with examples generally related to willing clients. You will find much about stress and burn-out, plus some sympathy for statutory workers who have to take the blame when things go wrong.

Looking for tangible results is problematic in any setting, though you may be surprised to know that some researchers find little difference in results between involuntary and voluntary clients – this was in a drug users' setting (Lurigo 2000, p.514).

There is nothing remarkable about the fact that someone who is not committed to his or her clients is not likely to have good results or experience much satisfaction, whereas the worker who enjoys the work will communicate the fact that he or she feels positive and believes the best of people – this is not the same as being unrealistic. A psychiatric colleague once said she thought that social workers' expectations of clients were generally too high – there is food for thought here – even though it may not be clear whether the psychiatrist was implying that her own professional body had lower sights!

RECOGNISING REWARDS

One of the interesting things about working with reluctant clients is that we do not always recognise the rewards when we receive them. Some of my own have only been seen years later:

- The young woman who said she was not going to ask for a loan any more.

- The client who asks for you personally, sometimes months after your last contact.

- The person who kept a promise not to make any more suicide bids without telling me.

- An excellent placement with foster carers for a young person who did *not* want to leave home, but needed to.

- Overhearing two adults who have learning difficulties saying they had been able to do things they never imagined in their lives – this was in a high security setting.

- Being allowed to make contact with someone's family, after a long period of estrangement, in order to see if reconciliation is possible.

PERSONAL GAIN

Some of the lasting rewards of working with people who do not want you are the things you learn about yourself and the world. Because such clients are not always so concerned with some of the social niceties as more 'motivated' people may be, they cut through your 'methods', 'assessments', 'goals' and other strategies like the proverbial knife through butter. I remember working with a student colleague during a shopping trip with a client. The latter had planned carefully, including where to shop, what the client needed, and how to ensure the trip wasn't too tiring – the client was somewhat infirm. Money was available so that he was not out of pocket. As the little group, the client, student and myself, progressed along the supermarket aisles, the client began to look more and more confused. Eventually I asked him what was wrong. He told me he didn't know what 'toiletries' were: the shopping list had in fact been made by the staff of the residential home in which he lived. Some people, and certainly not men of 80 years old in the poor area of the big city where the client grew up, did not buy toiletries. Trying to work as a team with other professionals leads us to all sorts of by-ways and learning points!

Then there are the colleagues, who are very special, not least because of the heartache we go through together. I respect particularly those whom I have seen overcoming the difficulties of working with people who did not want them. Even though the clients may be captives, making a working relationship cannot be prescribed by even the highest court in the land – it takes genuineness and skill.

When you are busy, reflecting on your work can suffer. Good supervision helps you to:

- think about what you have done

- think back over the details you may have missed

- consider how you tackled the different tasks

- remember what you did and how well you did it

- look at the final product as objectively as possible

- recognise your achievements and give yourself a pat on the back when you deserve it!

The importance of this obvious-sounding type of thinking and feeling is underlined by the fact that we are actually assessed on our ability to do it, as part of our professional training – in other words it is not simple, and is a skill that needs to be learned. The payoff is that it helps us to see the silver linings we all need. So here is a small reflective exercise to finish with:

· ·

Exercise: Reflection

In thinking back over the material in this book:

- What have you liked?

- What have you not liked?

- What have you found the most challenging aspect?

- Which aspects do you feel you need to discuss with someone?

- What action would you like to see in your own workplace?

- Whom could you enlist or consult to help you develop your skills?

- Have any of your hopes for this book been fulfilled?

· ·

ENDING WITH THE FLOWERS

I enjoy gardening, which is why the analogy of very small seeds turning into beautiful flowers means so much to me. Usually we won't see the flowers, but I should like to end by sharing a magic moment when I did.

A small baby of African/Caribbean heritage was placed by me with a white foster mother in a very white area. There were all sorts of reservations about the placement, but the foster mother loved the little girl so much, her physical and emotional care of the child was excellent, her support for the birth mother so genuine, that she was eventually allowed to adopt her. Some 30 years later a quality newspaper did a series on adoption, and my day was made one Saturday by reading a testimonial, which from description and photo was unmistakably the 'baby', speaking about her adoptive mother and the wonderful childhood she had experienced. Note:

I still believe that it is much better to place children with foster/adoptive parents of the same race as their own, if possible.

This book has been less about *how* to work with people and much more about *what* is important while doing so.

> Usually, work is inherently meaningful when something other than money is gained. (Martin 2000, p.478)

Summary

- Working with involuntary clients brings rewards in all sorts of different ways.
- We sometimes do not recognise rewards when we receive them.
- Some of our rewards come in the form of greater insight into people and situations.
- You may wish to reflect on the material in this book.
- I have had wonderful rewards.

FURTHER INFORMATION
Yourself!

References

Abbey, A., Cozzarelli, C., McLaughlin, K. and Harnish, R. (1987) 'The effects of clothing and dyad sex composition on perceptions of sexual intent: Do women and men evaluate these cues differently?' In K. Lindgren, M. Parkhill, W. George and C. Hendershot (2008) 'Gender differences in perceptions of sexual intent: A qualitative review and integration.' *Psychology of Women Quarterly* *32*, 4, 423–439.

Age Concern (2007) *My Home Life.* London: Age Concern.

Age Concern and British Institute of Human Rights (2009) *Older People and Human Rights: Research and Mapping Report.* London: Age Concern and British Institute of Human Rights.

Al-Mahmood, R. and McLoughlin, C. (2004) 'Re-learning through E-learning: Changing Conceptions of Teaching through Online Experience.' In R. Atkinson, C. McBeath, D. Jonas-Dwyer and R. Phillips (eds) *Beyond the Comfort Zone: Proceedings of the 21st ASCILITE Conference.* Perth: ASCILITE. Accessed on 7/10/09 at www.ascilite.org.au/conferences/perth04/procs/al-mahmood.html.

Al-Sayyad, A. and Adams, N. (2006) *Appearance and the Body.* Huntsville, AL: University of Alabama.

Argyle, M. (1988) *Bodily Communication.* Madison, WI: International Universities Press.

Argyle, M. (1996) *Bodily Communication.* London: Routledge.

Atkinson, J., Garner, H., Dyer, J. and Gilmour, W. (2002) 'Changes to leave of absence in Scotland: The views of patients.' *Journal of Forensic Psychiatry 13,* 315–328.

Axtell, R. (1998) *Gestures.* New York: Wiley.

Bayliss, M. (1998) 'Counselling Troubled Children Who Have Been Abused.' In Z. Bear (ed.) *Good Practice in Counselling Children Who Have Been Abused.* London: Jessica Kingsley Publishers.

Ben Asher, M. (2001) 'Spirituality and religion in social work practice.' *Social Work Today 7,* 1–7.

Beresford, P. (2007) *The Changing Roles and Tasks of Social Work from Service Users' Perspectives: A Literature Informed Discussion Paper.* London: Shaping Our Lives.

Bernard, C. and Baderin, D. (2002) *Diversity Checklist for the National Probation Service.* London: Home Office Communication Directorate.

Blatner, A. (2002) *The Hero Process.* Northfield, MN: Science Education Resource Center.Accessed on 3/11/09 at www.blatner.com/adam/psyntbk/hero.htm

Brandon, D. (1982) *The Trick of Being Ordinary: Notes for Volunteers and Students.* London: Mind.

Cade, B. (2007) 'Springs, Streams and Tributaries: A History of the Brief, Solution-focused Approach.' In S. Johnson (ed.) *Basic Assumptions about People and Problems.* Darwin: Solution Focused Counselling.

Cambridge Online Dictionary (2010) *Define.* Accessed on 8/03/10 at http://dictionary.cambridge. org/define.asp?key=63193.

Campaign for Freedom of Information (undated) *Your Rights to Personal Files.* London: Campaign for Freedom of Information. Accessed on 24/03/10 at www.cfoi.org.uk/persfilesintro.html.

Center for Rural Studies (1998) *Exercise Five: Non-verbal Expression.* Burlington, VT: The University of Vermont. Accessed on 6/08/09 at http://crs.uvm.edu/gopher/nerl/personal/comm/f.html.

Centre for Deaf Studies (2009) *10 Things to Know About Counselling a Deaf Person.* Bristol: University of Bristol.

Chambers (2003) *The Chambers Dictionary.* Edinburgh: Chambers Harrap.

Chartered Society of Physiotherapists (2009) *Professionalism, Personal Appearance and the Patient Experience.* London: Chartered Society of Physiotherapists. Accessed on 30/06/09 at www. csp.org.uk/uploads/documents/PD043%20Professionalism%20Appearance%20Patient%20 Experience_FV1.pdf.

Cingolani, J. (1993) *Working with Involuntary Clients: Practitioners' Perspectives and Strategies.* Edwardsville, IL: Southern Illinois University.

Commission for Social Care Inspection (2008) *Putting People First – Equality and Diversity Matters.* London: Commission for Social Care Inspection.

Cryer, J. (1990) 'Games people play in educational games, simulations and workshops: A transactional analysis perspective.' *Simulation Games for Learning 20,* 4, 368–377.

Curtin University of Technology (2006) *Good Practice World Wide – Teaching and Learning Resources.* Perth, Western Australia: Curtin University of Technology. Accessed on 12/11/08 at www.curtin. edu.au/online/netiquette.html (site no longer active).

Department of Health (2001) *Consent – What You Have a Right to Expect: A Guide for Adults.* London: Department of Health.

Department of Health (2007) *Human Rights in Health – A Framework for Local Action.* London: Department of Health.

Department of Health, Social Services and Public Safety, Northern Ireland (2003) *Racial Equality in Health and Social Care – Good Practice Guide.* Accessed on 31/11/09 at www.dhsspsni.gov.uk/ eq-raceeqhealth.

DePaulo, B., Kashy, D., Kirkendol, S. and Wyer, M. (1996) 'Lying in everyday life.' *Journal of Personality and Social Psychology 70,* 2, 979–995.

Diggins, M. (2004) *Teaching and Learning Communication Skills in Social Work Education.* London: Social Care Institute for Excellence.

Doel, M. and Shardlow, S. (1993) *Practice Learning.* Aldershot: Gower.

Doel, M and Shardlow, S. (2005) *Modern Social Work Practice.* Farnham: Ashgate.

Drinkwater, M. (2009) *Reaching a Compromise to Cross-dress in a Safe Environment.* Sutton: Community Care, 2 October 2009. Accessed on 30/10/09 at www.communitycare.co.uk/ articles/2009/10/02/112759/Risk-factor-helping-a-man-with-learning-disabilities-who.htm

Egan, G. (1994) *The Skilled Helper.* Pacific Grove, CA: Brooks/Cole.

Field, T. (1995) *Touch in Early Development.* Hillsdale, NJ: Erlbaum.

Finlay, L. (2001) *Groupwork in Occupational Therapy.* Cheltenham: Nelson Thornes.

Genera, M. and Kharrat, Y. (2000) *Learning the Culture as Well as the Words.* Saudi Arabia: King Khalid University/Pilgrims Ltd.

Gilligan, P. (2006) 'The role of religion and spirituality in social work practice: Views and experiences of social workers and students.' *British Journal of Social Work 36,* 4, 617–637.

Gloucestershire Hospitals NHS Trust (2003) *Management of Violence and Aggression.* Gloucester: Gloucestershire NHS Trust. Accessed on 16/10/09 at www.gloshospitals.nhs.uk/pdf/ boardpapers/archive/2003/boardmay03/item7manofvio.pdf.

Gough, D. (1993) *Child Abuse Interventions – A Review of the Research Literature.* London: University of Glasgow/HMSO.

Hamilton, R. and Dinat, N. (2006) *Juta's Counselling Handbook for Healthcare Professionals.* Cape Town: Juta.

Health and Safety Executive (2000) *Social Services: Social Inclusion and Elective Risk.* London: HMSO.

Hepworth, D., Rooney, R. and Larson, J. (1997) *Direct Social Work Practice: Theory and Skills.* Pacific Grove, CA: Brooks/Cole.

Hill, O. (2007) *Personality Disorder and Its Treatment.* London: Royal College of Psychiatrists. Accessed on 22/03/09 at www.rcpsych.ac.uk/campaigns/changingminds/mentaldisorders/ personalitydisorder.aspx

Hoffman, L. (1993) *Exchanging Voices: A Collaborative Approach to Family Therapy.* London: Karnac.

Hogg, M. and Vaughan, G. (2005) *Social Psychology.* Harlow: Prentice Hall.

Home Office (2008) *Personal Safety*. London: Home Office. Accessed 16/10/09 at www.crimereduction. homeoffice.gov.uk/personalsafety.htm.

Horner, N. and Kindred, M. (1997) *Using Crisis Intervention and Task-centred Theories in Social Work*. Birmingham: Open Learning Foundation.

Howe, D. (1990) 'The Client's View in Context.' In P. Carter, T. Jeffs and M. Smith (eds) *Social Work and Social Welfare Yearbook*. Milton Keynes: Open University Press.

Hunt, R. and Valentine, G. (2008) *Love Thy Neighbour: What People of Faith Really Think about Homosexuality*. London: Stonewall.

Hunter, M. and Struve, J. (1998) *The Ethical Use of Touch in Psychotherapy*. Thousand Oaks, CA: Sage.

Information Commissioner's Office (2008) *Data Protection Good Practice Note*. London: Information Commissioner. Accessed on 6/07/09 at www.ico.gov.uk/upload/documents/library/data_ protection/practical_application/gpn_recording_and_retaining_professional_opinions%20 v1_290408.pdf.

Keats, D. (2000) *Interviewing: A Practical Guide for Students and Professionals*. Buckingham: Open University Press.

Leishman, A., Bisset, J. and Walkden, C. (2005) *First Impressions: Can a Dentist's Facial Appearance Alter a Patient's Opinion of Them?* Glasgow: Glasgow Space Service. Accessed on 20/05/09 at http:// hdl.handle.net/1905/465.

Lewis, C. S. (2001) *The Screwtape Letters*. London: HarperCollins. (Original work published in 1942.)

Liberty (2008) *Marriage and Family*. London: Liberty. Accessed on 3/10/09 at www.yourrights.org.uk/ yourrights/the-rights-of-prisoners/marriage-and-family.html.

Lurigo, A. (2000) 'Social control and coercion in addiction treatment: Towards evidence-based policy and practice.' *Criminal Justice and Behaviour 27*, 4, 495–528.

Malpass, R. (1996) 'Face Recognition at the Interface of Psychology, Law and Medicine.' In H. Grad, A. Blanco and J. Georgas (eds) *Key Issues in Cross Cultural Psychology: Selected Papers from the Twelfth International Congress of the International Association for Cross-cultural Psychology*. Lisse: Swets and Zeitlinger.

Marlowe, D., Douglas B., Merikle, E., Kirby, K. *et al.* (2001) 'Multidimensional assessment of perceived treatment-entry pressures among substance abusers.' *Psychology of Addictive Behaviours 15*, 2, 97–108.

Martin, M. (2000) *Meaningful Work: Rethinking Professional Ethics*. Oxford: Oxford University Press.

Maslow, A. (1970) *Motivation and Personality*. New York: Harper and Row.

May, R. (1972) *Power and Innocence*. New York: Norton.

McDermott, T. and O'Connor, J. (1996) *Neuro-linguistic Programming and Health*. London: Thorsons.

McDonald, G. (2001) *Effective Interventions in Child Abuse and Neglect*. Chichester: Wiley.

Mehrabian, A. (1972) *Non-verbal Communication*. Chicago: Aldine Atherton.

Mill, J. and Gray, J. (2008) *On Liberty and Other Essays*. Oxford: Oxford University Press.

Miller, W. and Rollnick, S. (2004) *Motivational Interviewing*. New York: Guilford.

Mind (2009) *Mind Rights Guide 3: Consent to Treatment*. London: Mind.

Mooney, H. (2008) 'Do dress codes lead to discrimination?' *Nursing Times* 18 August, p.1.

Munro, E. (1995) 'The power of first impressions.' *Practice 7*, 3, 59–65.

Murray Parkes, C. (1983) *Bereavement*. New York: Basic Books.

Myers, I.B. and Myers, P.B. (1995) *Gifts Differing: Understanding Personality Type*. Mountain View, CA: Consulting Psychologists Press.

National Health Service (2007) *Dress Codes and Discrimination*. Leeds: NHS Employers. Accessed on 10/10/09 at www.nhsemployers.org/EmploymentPolicyAndPractice/EqualityAndDiversity/ Pages/DressCodesAndDiscrimination.aspx.

National Health Service Institute for Innovation and Improvement (undated) *Circumcision*. Newcastle upon Tyne: Sowerby Centre for Health Informatics.

Nursten, J. (1997) 'The end as a means to growth – within the social work relationship.' *Journal of Social Work Practice 11*, 2, 73–80.

Parker, P. (2009) *Professional Boundaries in Social Work: A Qualitative Study.* London: GSCC.

Pollio, D. (1995) 'Use of humour in crisis intervention.' *Families in Society: The Journal of Contemporary Human Services 76,* 6, 376–384.

Robinson, L. (2004) 'Beliefs, Values and Inter-ethnic Communication.' In S. Barrett, C. Komaromy, M. Robb and A. Rogers (eds) *Communication, Relationships and Care: A Reader.* London: Sage.

Rooney, R. (1992) *Strategies for Work with Involuntary Clients.* New York: Columbia University Press.

Royal College of Psychiatrists (2006) *Spirituality and Mental Health.* London: Spirituality and Psychiatry Special Interest Group.

Royal College of Psychiatrists (2007) *Self Harm.* London: Royal College of Psychiatrists.

Schulman, L. (1991) *Co-ordination and Child Protection.* Edinburgh: HMSO.

Seabury, A. (1976) 'The contract: Uses, abuses and limitations.' *Social Work,* 21 January, 16–21.

Seligman, M. (1995) *Learned Optimism.* New York: Free Press.

Smith, E. and Mackie, D. (2007) *Social Psychology.* Hove: Psychology Press.

Social Care Institute for Excellence (2008) *Promoting Dignity within the Law: Background to Dignity in Care and Its Relationship to Human Rights.* London: SCIE.

Struthers, J. (1999) 'An investigation into community psychiatric nurses' use of humour during client interactions.' *Journal of Advance Nursing 29,* 5, 1197–1204.

TOPSS (2004) *National Occupational Standards for Social Work England.* Leeds: TOPSS.

Trotter, C. (1990) 'Probation can work: A research study using volunteers.' *Australian Journal of Social Work 43,* 2, 13–18.

Trotter, C. (1996) 'The impact of different supervision practices in community corrections.' *Australian and New Zealand Journal of Criminology 28,* 2, 29–46.

Trotter, C. (2006) *Working with Involuntary Clients.* Crows Nest, Western Australia: Allen and Unwin.

Tschudin, V. (1997) 'Counselling for loss and bereavement.' *British Journal of Social Work 27,* 471–473.

Usiskin, J. (1998) *Working with Disability.* Ely: Fenman.

Wainwright, G. (2003) *Body Language.* London: Hodder.

Webb, S.A. (2000) 'The politics of social work: Power and subjectivity.' *Critical Social Work 1,* 2, 1–2.

Williams, D. (1997) *Communication Skills in Practice: A Practical Guide for Health Professionals.* London: Jessica Kingsley Publishers.

Williams, D. (2001) *The Social Work Process.* Wrexham: Glyndŵr University.

Wisconsin Department of Health and Family Services (2002) *Strategies for Initiating Meaningful, Quality Home Visits with People who have Dementia.* Madison, WI: Department of Health and Family Services. Accessed on 1/10/09 at www.dhs.wisconsin.gov/aging/dementia/visits.pdf.

World Health Organization (2008) *Definitions.* Geneva: WHO.

Yatchmenoff, D. (2008) 'A Closer Look at Client Engagement: Understanding and Assessing Engagement from the Perspectives of Workers and Clients in Non-voluntary Child Protective Service Cases.' In M. Calder (ed.) *The Carrot or the Stick: Towards Effective Practice with Involuntary Clients in Safeguarding Children Work.* Lyme Regis: Russell House.

Zuck, R. (1997) *The Speaker's Quote Book.* Grand Rapids, MI: Kregel Publications.

Subject Index

Author Index